Joint Doctrine Note (JDN) 1-13, Security Force Assistance (SFA), is a pre-doctrinal publication that presents generally agreed to fundamental guidance for joint forces conducting SFA. It is considered a part of the initiation stage of the joint doctrine development process. Once extant and validated best practices and procedures are common across the operating forces, appropriate principles and guidance are incorporated into existing joint doctrine hierarchy or, if required, a new joint publication (JP).

Despite the importance of its national mission, SFA does not have a dedicated JP and existing joint doctrine makes only occasional references to it. To address this joint doctrinal gap, J-7 developed the following JDN for the joint force's consideration. Although this JDN has not been through the joint doctrine development system as described in Chairman of the Joint Chiefs of Staff Instruction 5120.02C, *Joint Doctrine Development System,* it draws on both contemporary and historical experiences to describe the documented best practices currently in use across the joint force. It also connects SFA to United States national strategy and policy guidance, discusses organization and planning for SFA, and provides considerations for conducting SFA activities.

The guidance in this JDN is not authoritative. If conflicts arise between the contents of this JDN and the contents of a JP, the JP will take precedence for the activities of joint forces unless the Chairman of the Joint Chiefs of Staff, normally in coordination with the other members of the Joint Chiefs of Staff, has provided more current and specific guidance.

In order to establish the full context for SFA, this JDN includes some content found in other references. It is our intent to modify portions of the text as users throughout the joint force study, apply, and comment on this JDN. We welcome your feedback concerning this JDN.

GEORGE J. FLYNN
Lieutenant General, USMC
Director for Joint Force Development

Intentionally Blank

PREFACE

1. Purpose—What?

A joint doctrine note (JDN) is a pre-doctrinal publication that presents common fundamental guidance and is part of the initiation stage of the joint doctrine development process. Although there is some agreement over contributions, this JDN does not necessarily describe a position of consensus across joint forces. Once extant and validated best practices and procedures are common across the operating forces, appropriate principles and guidance are incorporated into existing joint doctrine hierarchy or, if required, a new joint publication (JP).

2. Purpose—Context?

The importance of a unified United States Government (USG) effort in the planning, execution, and assessment of security force assistance (SFA) has grown both within the Department of Defense (DOD) and across the USG. Therefore, the joint force contribution to SFA should be consistent with the Office of the Secretary of Defense security cooperation policy to achieve combatant command theater campaign plans objectives and nested with a comprehensive USG unified action plan. This JDN was prepared under the direction of the Director for Joint Force Development. It sets forth guidance for joint activities and performance of the Services in SFA activities. It also provides guidance for use by the combatant commanders in preparing their appropriate plans. While this JDN does not restrict the authority of the joint force commander to organize forces, commanders must understand that authorities associated with conducting SFA training and equipping of security forces are governed by US law. As such, commanders should seek legal counsel prior to executing SFA missions.

3. Purpose—How?

a. Though not authoritative, the guidance within this publication is relevant to SFA activities of the Joint Staff, commanders of combatant commands, subunified commands, joint task forces, subordinate components of these commands, the Services, and DOD agencies in support of joint operations.

b. Commanders of forces operating as part of a multinational force should follow multinational doctrine and procedures ratified by the United States. For doctrine and procedures not ratified by the US, commanders should evaluate and follow the multinational force's doctrine and procedures, where applicable and consistent with US law, regulations, and doctrine. If conflicts arise between the contents of this JDN and the contents of JPs, the JPs will take precedence unless otherwise directed by the Chairman of the Joint Chiefs of Staff.

c. This JDN consists of four chapters:

(1) Chapter I. Defines SFA as an integral part of three key DOD concepts: security cooperation, the range of military operations, and instruments of national power.

(2) Chapter II. Describes the roles of DOD, the Department of State, United States Agency for International Development, and other US departments and agencies in conducting SFA.

(3) Chapter III. Outlines SFA goals, imperatives, functional considerations in security force development, security force frameworks, theater planning considerations, and SFA assessment.

(4) Chapter IV. Examines employment principles, tools, and techniques used in conducting SFA activities.

d. This JDN is designed to supplement the approved joint doctrine contained in many JPs including JP 3-0, *Joint Operations;* JP 3-24, *Counterinsurgency Operations;* JP 3-22, *Foreign Internal Defense;* JP 3-26, *Counterterrorism*; and JP 3-07, *Stability Operations.*

TABLE OF CONTENTS

GLOSSARY

FIGURE

EXECUTIVE SUMMARY
COMMANDER'S OVERVIEW

- **Presents an Overview of Security Force Assistance**

- **Describes Organization and Responsibilities**

- **Explains Planning for Security Force Assistance**

- **Discusses Security Force Assistance Activities**

Overview of Security Force Assistance

General

Security force assistance (SFA) is the set of Department of Defense (DOD) activities that contribute to unified action by the United States Government (USG) to support the development of capability and capacity of foreign security forces (FSF) and supporting institutions. FSF are all organizations and personnel under host nation (HN) control that have a mission of protecting the HN's sovereignty from internal as well as external threats. SFA activities are primarily used to assist an HN in defending against internal and transnational threats to stability (i.e., supporting foreign internal defense [FID], counterterrorism, counterinsurgency [COIN], or stability operations).

Relationship to Other Security Cooperation Related Activities and Programs

Security cooperation (SC) activities are undertaken by DOD to encourage and enable international partners to work with the US to achieve strategic objectives. SFA is a subset of SC activities that develop and sustain HN FSF capabilities.

Security assistance (SA) refers to a group of programs, authorized by the Foreign Assistance Act of 1961, as amended, the Arms Export Control Act of 1976, as amended, Title 22, United States Code, as amended, or other related statutes, by which the US provides defense articles, military training, and other defense-related services to foreign nations by grant, loan, credit, or cash sales in furtherance of national policies and objectives. DOD administered SA programs are a subset of SC and normally are required to conduct SFA activities, but some SA programs do not contribute to SFA. SA programs are one means to enable SFA activities via a group of statutory programs funded and authorized by the DOS and

---

administered by the DOD Defense Security Cooperation Agency.

Foreign Assistance. DOD may use SFA activities as part of USG foreign assistance efforts. Foreign assistance is a broad category of USG assistance to foreign nations.

Security sector reform (SSR) is the set of policies, plans, programs, and activities that a government undertakes to improve the way it provides safety, security, and justice. SFA contributes to the DOD role in SSR initiatives.

Stability Operations is an overarching term encompassing various US Armed Forces missions, tasks, and activities conducted outside the US in coordination with other instruments of national power to maintain or reestablish a safe and secure environment, provide essential governmental services, emergency infrastructure reconstruction, and humanitarian relief. SFA supports the stability tasks of establishing civil security and civil control.

COIN is the comprehensive civilian and military effort undertaken to defeat an insurgency and to address the population's core grievances. SFA activities conducted during US COIN operations in an HN should support HN COIN objectives.

FID is the participation by civilian and military agencies of a government in any of the action programs taken by another government, or other designated organization, to free and protect its society from subversion, lawlessness, insurgency, terrorism, and other threats to their security. SFA and DOD FID are both subsets of SC, but neither SFA nor FID are subsets of one another, because SFA activities serve other purposes beyond internal defense.

Security Force Assistance Activities and Instruments of National Power

Effective use of SFA activities requires a strategic perspective on the development of FSF, including acknowledgment of theater and global objectives. While SFA activities are important for improving the capability and capacity of HN's security forces and their supporting institutions, for the long term, a USG partnership with an HN government normally benefits as much from the developments spawned by the economic, diplomatic, and informational instruments as from the military.

Organization and Responsibilities

Department of State is responsible for planning and implementing the foreign policy of the US. The chief of mission, typically the ambassador, is the principal officer in charge of US diplomatic missions and US offices abroad, which the Secretary of State has designated as diplomatic in nature.

As the lead US foreign affairs agency, **Department of State (DOS)** coordinates, represents, and implements US foreign policy. The Bureau of Political-Military Affairs is the DOS's principal link to DOD.

As statutorily mandated, the **chief of mission (COM)** directs and supervises all activities in country and coordinates the resources and programs of the USG through the country team with the exception of employees under the command of a US area military commander, and other exceptions consistent with existing statutes and authorities.

Each **[US embassy] country team** handles the following issues: commercial, resource, and financial issues; defense issues; agricultural matters; legal and immigration matters; and, developmental and humanitarian aid matters.

The **geographic combatant commander (GCC)** is the US military representative to international and US national agencies and is the single point of contact for military matters within the area of responsibility. The GCC is responsible for planning, conducting, and assessing SC activities, and for planning and conducting military support to stability operations, humanitarian assistance, and disaster relief, as directed.

Special operations forces, normally contribute to the SFA effort under operational control of the commander, theater special operations commander, or a commander, special operations component command, who has primary responsibility to plan and supervise the execution of special operations in support of the GCC or a subordinate joint force commander, respectively.

Planning for Security Force Assistance

Considerations for Security Force Assistance Planning

Theater Campaign Plan (TCP). Theater campaign planning should incorporate country planning, and the GCC's country plans or in some cases regional plans, should align with the COM's goals because TCP activities and resource investments typically occur at the country level. Senior defense officials/defense attachés, supported by the combatant commands' SC offices, help coordinate and align country planning with COM goals.

Country Plan. A country plan provides guidance to various DOD elements who implement and support planned SC activities. Country plans provide the roadmap of specific engagement activities that a GCC intends to conduct over one to three years. Development of plans that include SFA activities should include specific and measurable objectives and assessment criteria.

Security Force Assistance Goals

The ultimate goal of SFA activities is to create FSF that are competent, capable, sustainable, committed, and confident, and have a security apparatus tied to regional stability. Regional security may partly be achieved in partnership with an HN by developing its ability to deter and defend against military aggression by its neighbors and to combat lawlessness, subversion, insurgency, and terrorist threats.

Imperatives

The following imperatives are essential to SFA activities, and they have universal application for the numerous SC activities and larger-scale Service/joint operations and missions supported by SFA activities. They are understand the operational environment; ensure unity of effort; provide effective leadership; build legitimacy; synchronized information; sustainability; support HN ownership; incorporate principles of good governance and respect for human rights; link security and justice; foster transparency; and do no harm.

Security Force Functions

Security forces perform three generic functions: executive, generating, and operating. The executive function includes strategic direction that provides oversight, policy, and resources for the FSF generating and operating functions. FSF generating forces refer to the capability and capacity of the FSF to organize, train, equip, and build operating force units. FSF operating forces form operational capabilities through the use of concepts similar to the US joint functions to achieve FSF security objectives.

Foreign Security Force Development Tasks

SFA activities normally use the tasks of organize, train, equip, rebuild/build, and advise (OTERA) to develop the functional capabilities required by the FSF. Through a baseline assessment of the subject FSF, and considering US interests and objectives, planners can determine which OTERA tasks will be required to build the proper capability and capacity levels within the various units of the FSF.

General Theater Planning Considerations	SFA should be integrated into the specific operation or campaign plans in all phases, not just as an afterthought for the stabilize and enable civil authority phases following combat operations. Early planning should involve joint and interagency partners, whenever possible, to marshal and focus US capabilities and maximize capabilities of the HN and its allies.
Security Force Assistance Assessment	Appropriate subject matter experts should assess FSF capabilities and capacity based on the USG anticipated end state. From the baseline, assessment continues throughout FSF development to measure the effectiveness of SFA efforts and levels of FSF developmental efforts.

Security Force Assistance Activities

SFA activities are part of the unified actions of the geographic combatant commander and require interagency coordination.	Interagency coordination for SC such as SFA activities is normally led by the COM and coordinated through the country team. SFA activities may be conducted with FSF through large joint/Service task forces as well as through smaller civilian military teams.
Employment Factors	As in planning, several areas deserve special attention when discussing employment of forces in SFA activities. These include information operations impact; psychological impact, intelligence support, force selection; operational environment and employment tasking of SFA forces; public information; logistics support; force protection; operational security; communications security; and lessons learned.
Human Rights	HN personnel should be vetted prior to engagement to ensure no members of the training audience have violated human rights. No assistance shall be furnished under the Foreign Assistance Act or the Arms Export Control Act to any unit of the security forces of a foreign country if the Secretary of State has credible information that such unit has committed a gross violation of human rights.
Countering Insider Threats	Eliminating and/or minimizing the insider threat, especially by proper preparation and training of forces, is critical to mission success. However, more stringent force protection controls and measures that are overtly heavy handed must be well balanced yet culturally sensitive enough to not send the wrong message to the very people and organizations the US is trying to assist.

Other Operations and Activities

There are activities which are part of overall DOD security cooperation efforts that provide valuable opportunities for engagements between the US and HNs, but fall outside the scope of SFA. Regardless, these additional activities should be planned and executed by GCCs using DOD individuals and units, and will have significant impact and effect on SFA activities.

CONCLUSION

The guidance in this joint doctrine note is not authoritative.

Joint Doctrine Note (JDN) 1-13, *Security Force Assistance,* is a pre-doctrinal publication that presents generally agreed to fundamental guidance for joint forces conducting SFA. Although this JDN has not been through the joint doctrine development system as described in Chairman of the Joint Chiefs of Staff Instruction 5120.02C, *Joint Doctrine Development System,* it draws on both contemporary and historical experiences to describe the documented best practices currently in use across the joint force.

CHAPTER I
OVERVIEW OF SECURITY FORCE ASSISTANCE

"The US will work closely with allies and partners to ensure collective capability and capacity for securing common interests...SFA [security force assistance] is a core task for the Military Departments."

Defense Planning Guidance, Fiscal Years 14-18

1. General

a. Security force assistance (SFA) is the set of Department of Defense (DOD) activities that contribute to unified action by the United States Government (USG) to support the development of capability and capacity of foreign security forces (FSF) and supporting institutions. FSF are all organizations and personnel under host nation (HN) control that have a mission of protecting the HN's sovereignty from internal as well as external threats. Elements of FSF normally include full-time, reserve, or auxiliary military forces, police, corrections personnel, border guards (to include the Coast Guard) or other similar capabilities at the local through national levels. Institutions that support FSF include government ministries or departments, academies, training centers, logistics centers, and other similar activities from the local through national levels, and they provide the supporting doctrine, organization, training, materiel, leadership, education, personnel, facilities, and policy for the FSF.

b. SFA supports the professionalization and sustainable development of the capability and capacity of an HN's FSF and their supporting institutions, and those FSF that are part of intergovernmental organizations (IGOs). SFA can be used during any phase of an operation and across the range of military operations.

c. SFA activities are primarily used to assist an HN in defending against internal and transnational threats to stability (i.e., supporting foreign internal defense [FID], counterterrorism, counterinsurgency [COIN], or stability operations). SFA activities may be used to assist an HN defend against external threats or help contribute to multinational operations; and help develop or reform another country's security forces or supporting institutions. SFA also may be used to develop security forces of an IGO. In all cases, SFA activities are conducted with, through, and by the FSF to improve their capacity and capabilities through organize, train, equip, rebuild/build, and advise (OTERA).

d. SFA also contributes to DOD's role in USG efforts to support HN security sector reform (SSR). SFA often supports security cooperation (SC) initiatives, however, SC activities, dedicated to non-security sector such as bilateral meetings, other engagement opportunities, or some civil-military operations (e.g., populace control measures for internally displaced persons or refugees) fall outside the scope of SFA.

See Chapter III, "Planning for Security Force Assistance," for a more detailed discussion of strategic guidance.

2. Relationship to Other Security Cooperation Related Activities and Programs

a. **SC.** SC activities and programs may be applied across the range of military operations. SC activities are undertaken by DOD to encourage and enable international partners to work with the US to achieve strategic objectives. It includes all DOD interactions with foreign defense and security establishments, including all DOD-administered security assistance (SA) programs, that involves all DOD interactions with foreign defense establishments to build defense relationships that promote specific US interests, develop allied and friendly military capabilities for self-defense and multinational operations, and provide US forces with peacetime and contingency access to an HN. SC is an amalgamation of all the means by which DOD encourages and enables other countries and organizations to work with the US through Service/joint operations and activities to achieve strategic objectives. **SC has an overarching functional relationship with SA, FID, SFA, SSR, and all DOD security related activities.** SFA is a subset of SC activities that develop and sustain HN FSF capabilities.

(1) SC is a key element of global and theater shaping activities. Geographic combatant commanders (GCCs) shape their areas of responsibility (AORs) through SC activities by employing military forces to complement and reinforce other instruments of national power. One of the goals of SC activities is to reduce the causes of a potential crisis before a situation deteriorates and US military intervention is required.

(2) The active military engagement of the US Armed Forces with an HN's security forces or defense institutions element in an open manner facilitates access and influence, as well as building strategic partnerships. As a subset of SC, SFA is the set of military activities tied directly to development of the security capability and capacity of an FSF in support of US interests.

b. **SA.** SA refers to a group of programs, authorized by the Foreign Assistance Act of 1961, as amended, the Arms Export Control Act of 1976, as amended, Title 22, United States Code (USC), as amended, or other related statutes, by which the US provides defense articles, military training, and other defense-related services to foreign nations by grant, loan, credit, or cash sales in furtherance of national policies and objectives. DOD does not administer every SA program. For example, the United States Agency for International Development (USAID) administers the Economic Support Fund and the Department of State (DOS) administers direct commercial sales licensed under the Arms Export Control Act. Whether administered by DOD or DOS, SA programs support the development of FSF, especially when used as part of SFA activities supporting a Service/joint operation/mission, which is part of routine SC activities, a FID program, a COIN operation, or stability operation. DOD administered SA programs are a subset of SC and normally are required to conduct SFA activities, but some SA programs do not contribute to SFA.

(1) Examples of DOD administered SA activities are the foreign military sales (FMS) program, the foreign military financing (FMF) program, and the international military education and training (IMET) program.

(2) SA programs are one means to enable SFA activities via a group of statutory programs funded and authorized by the DOS and administered by the DOD Defense Security Cooperation Agency. These SA programs provide support and enable SFA activities.

c. **Foreign Assistance.** DOD may use SFA activities as part of USG foreign assistance efforts. Foreign assistance is a broad category of USG assistance to foreign nations that range from the sale of military equipment and support for FID to donations of food and medical supplies to aid survivors of natural and man-made disasters; and that may be provided through SA, development assistance, or humanitarian assistance.

d. **SSR.** SSR is the set of policies, plans, programs, and activities that a government undertakes to improve the way it provides safety, security, and justice. The overall objective is to provide these services in a way that promotes effective and legitimate governance that is transparent, accountable to civilian authority, and responsive to the needs of the public. SSR is an umbrella term that includes integrated activities in support of defense and armed forces reform. This includes civilian management and oversight; justice, police, corrections, and intelligence reform; national security planning and strategy support; border management; and disarmament, demobilization, and reintegration (DDR). SSR may include measures for the reduction of armed violence. SFA contributes to the DOD role in SSR initiatives.

e. **Stability Operations.** Stability operations is an overarching term encompassing various US Armed Forces missions, tasks, and activities conducted outside the US in coordination with other instruments of national power to maintain or reestablish a safe and secure environment, provide essential governmental services, emergency infrastructure reconstruction, and humanitarian relief. SFA supports the stability tasks of establishing civil security and civil control. This assistance may improve the capability and capacity of FSF of an HN currently under no immediate threat, paramilitary forces encountering an insurgency, or advising FSF in major combat operations against an external threat.

f. **COIN**

(1) COIN is the comprehensive civilian and military effort undertaken to defeat an insurgency and to address the population's core grievances. COIN is primarily diplomatic and incorporates a wide range of activities of which security is only one. Successful COIN operations require unified action, and should include all appropriate HN, US, and multinational agencies or actors. COIN efforts protect the population, defeat the insurgents, reinforce HN legitimacy, and build HN capabilities. COIN efforts include, but are not limited to, political, diplomatic, economic, health, financial, intelligence, law enforcement, legal, informational, military, paramilitary, psychological, and civic actions.

(2) **Relationship of SFA to COIN.** US COIN doctrine incorporates a wide range of activities, of which security is only one. Throughout US COIN operations, the efforts to build HN security forces are through SFA activities using OTERA tasks. SFA supports USG efforts to transition responsibilities to the HN. It is the developmental activity of the security line of effort during COIN operations that provides the HN a means of defeating future insurgencies by their own means. SFA activities conducted during US COIN operations in an HN should support HN COIN objectives.

g. **FID.** FID is the participation by civilian and military agencies of a government in any of the action programs taken by another government, or other designated organization, to free and protect its society from subversion, lawlessness, insurgency, terrorism, and other threats to their security.

(1) US Armed Forces support to FID should focus on the operational assistance to HN personnel and collaborative planning with inter-organizational and HN authorities to anticipate, preclude, and counter these threats. FID supports the HN's internal defense and development (IDAD) programs. Traditionally, FID builds capability and capacity of HN FSF to identify, deter, and defeat an insurgency through SC programs and operations. FID can assist in defeating an active insurgency, late into or post phase I (strategic defensive), if it cannot deter it by creating an environment that makes the organized movement or insurgency irrelevant. US FID programs may address other threats to the internal stability of an HN, such as civil disorder, illicit drug trafficking, and terrorism. While FID is a legislatively mandated core activity of special operations forces (SOF), conventional forces (CF) also generate and employ organic capabilities to conduct these activities.

(2) **Relationship Between SFA and FID.** SFA activities are conducted primarily, but not exclusively, to assist HNs defend against internal and transnational threats to stability. SFA and DOD FID are both subsets of SC, but neither SFA nor FID are subsets of one another, because SFA activities serve other purposes beyond internal defense. SFA, SA, and FID have functional not hierarchical relationships. FID programs, with established objectives in support of the HN IDAD, provide the ways (i.e., planned sequence of actions to achieve objectives), while SFA activities, including required SA, provide the SFA-qualified personnel, material, and equipment for training and/or advisory assistance to FSF from the tactical unit up to the ministerial level. Also, if an HN has an SSR requirement as part of the IDAD, SFA activities would support SSR as part of FID. SFA tasks include OTERA, and may include specific SC activities such as FMS or combined exercises. However, there are no specific tasks that define FID. FID can be defined as purpose behind a given SFA task. For example, the USG could provide military hardware to an HN via FMS in order to enable the HN to defend itself from external threats only (consider US arms sales to Japan); this is an example of SFA, but not FID. The USG could sell the same major end items to another country for the purpose of combating insurgents as well as defending against external threats (consider US arms sales to Israel); this would be an example of SFA as well as FID. There are a number of non-military tasks such as support to HN criminal justice systems and efforts to combat terrorist financing that support FID, but are not SFA tasks.

(a) USG FID must support an HN's IDAD strategy and programs. FID military operations normally support other instruments of national power through a variety of activities and tasks that enhance the HN IDAD program. SFA provides many, but not necessarily all, of the activities through which FID can be accomplished. Other SC initiatives dedicated to the non-security sector that may support FID, such as bilateral meetings or civil affairs activities, fall outside the scope of SFA. Again, SFA activities are conducted with, through, and by FSF, and the portion of SFA activities supporting an HN's efforts to counter threats from subversion, lawlessness, and insurgency support FID.

(b) SFA normally provides many, but not necessarily all, of the activities through which FID can be accomplished, dependent upon the contribution of interagency and multinational partners. Also, SFA activities may have to support the development of non-military security forces and their supporting institutions; and to the extent authorized by law, the DOD shall be prepared to provide capabilities to do the following:

<u>1</u>. Support and coordinate with other USG agencies that are leading USG efforts to support non-defense ministry security forces and their supporting institutions.

<u>2</u>. Advise and support the training of foreign paramilitary security forces such as border and coastal control forces, counterterrorist forces, and paramilitary or special police forces at all levels, in conjunction with other USG agencies.

<u>3</u>. Support the training of HN civil police in individual and collective tasks in contested environments when other USG agency trainers and advisors are unable to do so. Coordinate the transition of responsibilities for such training and advisory duties to other USG agencies as the security environment allows.

(c) In addition to providing basic security, a major joint force role in FID or stability operations may be to support an HN's SSR, the broad set of policies, plans, programs, and activities that a government undertakes to improve the way it provides safety, security, and justice to the indigenous population. SFA activities, at the ministerial level and down to the tactical unit level, if necessary, can provide the activities for an HN attaining and sustaining the transformational objectives of SSR. However, in the absence of a FID requirement in an HN IDAD, but for positive governance and legitimacy, SSR may be accomplished through SFA activities and SA under SC.

For more details regarding SSR, see Joint Publication (JP) 3-07, Stability Operations, *Appendix C, Security Sector Reform.*

For further guidance on FID, refer to JP 3-22, Foreign Internal Defense. *For further guidance on SOF involvement in FID, refer to JP 3-05,* Special Operations.

h. **SFA.** The focus of other FID operations is typically the population; in contrast, the focus of SFA activities is FSF. These activities occur in support of the achievement of specific objectives shared by the HN and the USG. The purposes of SFA activities are to create, maintain, or enhance a sustainable capability or capacity to achieve a desired end state. Most importantly, these purposes distinguish SFA activities from other SC activities, although they may appear identical to the population we are serving, and to the forces executing them on the ground. SC activities undertaken to gain access, to influence diplomatic/political action, but which do not enhance the HN capability or capacity, are not SFA. Other USG departments and agencies focus on those forces assigned to other ministries (or their equivalents) such as interior, justice, or intelligence services.

i. **SFA Personnel Considerations.** DOD conducts SFA activities with the appropriate combination of CF, SOF, civilian expeditionary workforce (CEW), multinational forces, and contract personnel, which collectively provide capability to execute missions and activities.

j. **SFA for non-defense ministry security forces and their supporting institutions.** If required to support the development of the capability and capacity of non-defense ministry security forces, such as the police and their supporting institutions, and to the extent authorized by law, DOD is prepared to employ the requisite task-organized capabilities to affect the following:

(1) Support and coordinate with other interagency partners leading and supporting USG efforts to support development of the capability and capacity of non-defense ministry security forces and their supporting institutions.

(2) Advise and support the training of foreign paramilitary security forces such as border and coastal control forces, counterterrorist forces, and paramilitary or special police forces at all levels.

(3) Support the training of HN civil police in individual and collective tasks in hostile or uncertain operational environments when trainers and advisors from other interagency partners are unable to do so.

(4) Coordinate the transition of responsibilities for such training and advisory duties to other interagency partners when the security environment allows.

3. The Range of Military Operations

a. SFA activities are conducted across the range of military operations from peace through war supporting Service and joint operations/missions. Significant SC activities and military engagements are routinely conducted worldwide during peacetime phase 0 (shaping) through the GCCs theater campaign plans (TCPs). Some of those SC activities are likely to include, for example, SFA activities supporting FID programs or an SSR effort in the lower range of the conflict continuum. Timely and effective execution of relevant SFA activities in phase 0 and phase I (deter) may prevent the requirement for US forces to conduct phase II (seize initiative) and phase III (dominate) operations. Execution of relevant SFA activities in phases 0 and I contribute to the HN's organic capability for managing destabilizing events. These activities provide effective HN security forces for US and multinational forces to partner with if required to reestablish stability.

b. Joint forces must have the ability to conduct SFA and associated OTERA tasks throughout the operational environment. Planners should address SFA requirements throughout all phases of an operation/campaign. (See Figure I-1.)

For more information on the range of military operations, refer to JP 3-0, Joint Operations.

4. Security Force Assistance Activities and Instruments of National Power

a. Effective use of SFA activities requires a strategic perspective on the development of FSF, including acknowledgment of theater and global objectives, which is why GCCs formally forecast their annual SC requirements (including SFA) after coordination with country teams in their AORs. DOD components should work with DOS and other interagency partners to develop comprehensive, requirements-driven strategies that can then

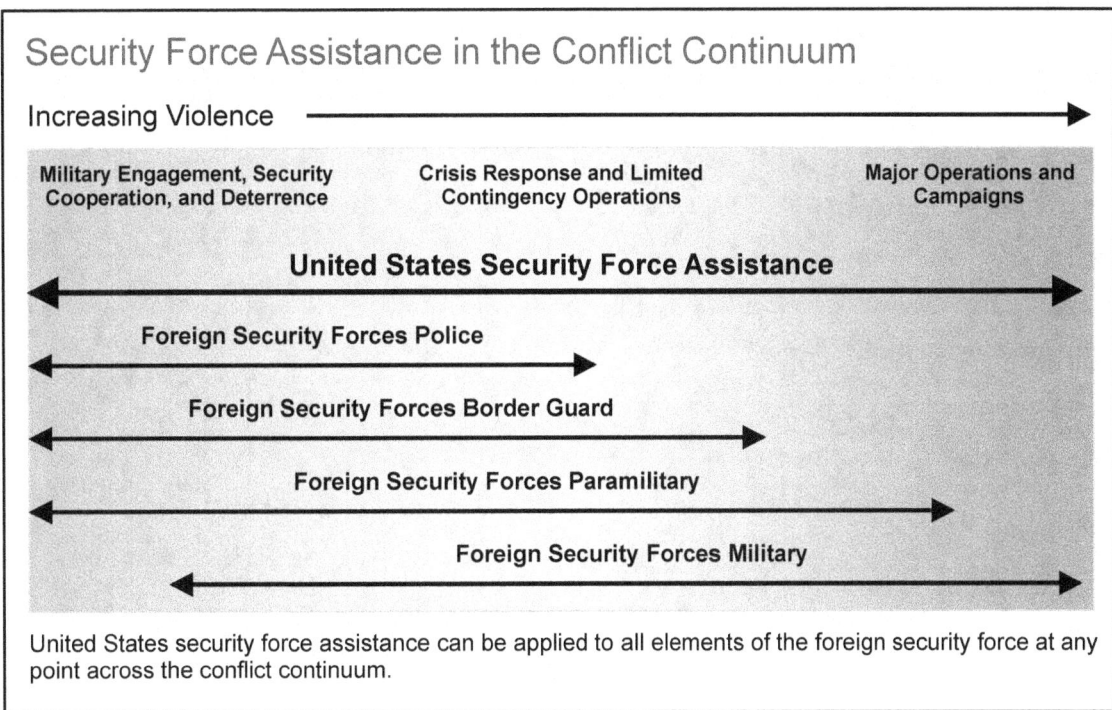

Figure I-1. Security Force Assistance in the Conflict Continuum

be resourced by the full complement of USG assistance programs that likely include all the instruments of national power. For example, Title 22, USC, funds for FMF and IMET are part of DOS foreign operations budget, and not entirely governed by DOD priorities, so interagency coordination can link resources to overarching goals, and creation of operational roadmaps for long term SC where it is required. An effective global approach to improving numerous HNs' security programs necessitates an innovation based on comprehensive requirements-based strategies and authorities that provide legitimate, lethal, and stabilizing capabilities to the FSF.

b. DOD employs US capabilities to aid HNs in preparing for and conducting operations to mitigate threats to their national, regional, or global security and stability, because it is in the best interests of the USG. While SFA activities are important for improving the capability and capacity of HN's security forces and their supporting institutions, for the long-term, a USG partnership with an HN government normally benefits as much from the developments spawned by the economic, diplomatic, and informational instruments as from the military.

Intentionally Blank

CHAPTER II
ORGANIZATION AND RESPONSIBILITIES

1. General

a. **Scope.** This chapter describes the SFA relationship among DOD, DOS, USAID, and other USG organizations, primarily at the country team level. It also provides background on the various sources of SFA guidance that serve to influence not only SFA activities but also the overall engagement strategy with the partner nation (PN).

b. **Whole-of-Government Approach.** Military engagement, SC, and deterrence missions, tasks, and actions encompass a wide range of actions where the military instrument of national power is tasked to support other interagency partners and cooperate with IGOs (e.g., United Nations [UN], North Atlantic Treaty Organization) and other countries to protect and enhance national security interests, deter conflict, and set conditions for future contingency operations. These activities generally occur continuously in all GCCs' AORs regardless of other ongoing contingencies, major operations, or campaigns. SFA activities that strengthen the capability and capacity of a PN's security forces occur within the overall engagement strategy.

c. DOS is frequently the major player in these types of activities. DOD, the GCCs, and military attachés work with the chiefs of the US diplomatic missions around the world and with the US DOS regional and functional bureaus, and other government branches and departments, to coordinate activities in support of national security objectives.

d. While the executive branch of USG, under the authority of the President, has the responsibility for conducting foreign policy and defending the country, the US Congress has constitutional mandate and authority to fund and legislate. Consequently, the US Congress provides oversight of SFA activities and allocates resources under strict guidelines and implementation instructions. As a result, the funding authorities (the means) for SFA activities constrain departments and governmental bureaus on how, where, and under what circumstances SFA activities occur. Figure II-1 depicts SFA coordination.

2. National Organization

a. **DOS.** DOS is responsible for planning and implementing the foreign policy of the US. As the lead US foreign affairs agency, DOS coordinates, represents, and implements US foreign policy. The Secretary of State, the ranking member of the Cabinet, is the President's principal advisor on foreign policy and the person chiefly responsible for US representation abroad.

b. DOS is organized into regional and functional bureaus. The six regional bureaus, responsible to the Under Secretary for Political Affairs, formulate and implement regional foreign policy and bilateral policy toward each individual country of the world.

c. The assistant secretaries of the regional bureaus and offices advise the Under Secretary for Political Affairs and guide the operation of the US diplomatic missions within

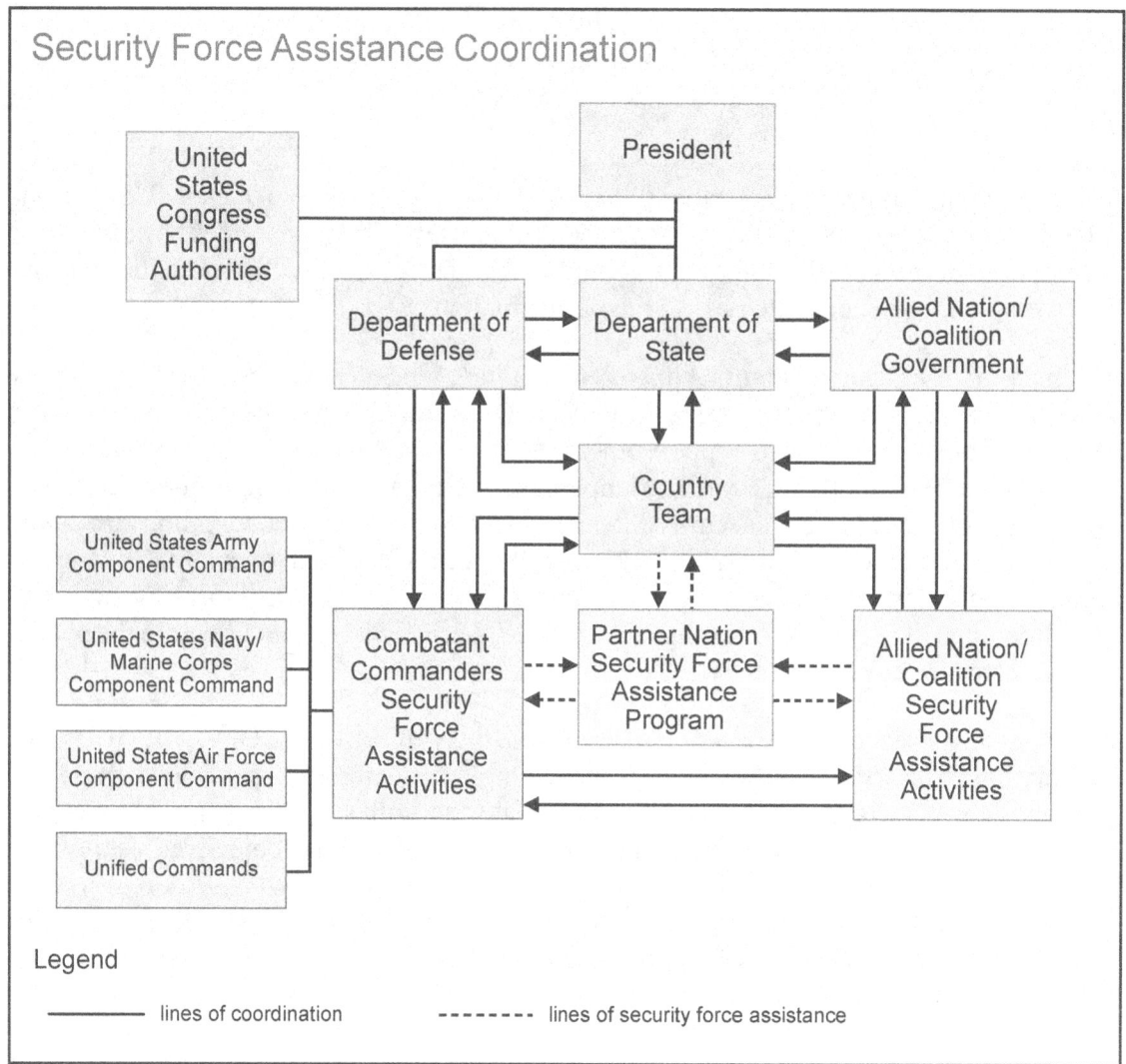

Figure II-1. Security Force Assistance Coordination

their regional jurisdiction. Deputy assistant secretaries, office directors, post management officers, and country desk officers assist them. These officials work closely with US embassies and consulates overseas and with foreign embassies in Washington, DC.

d. Headed by the Assistant Secretary of State for International Organizational Affairs, a seventh bureau, responsible to the Under Secretary for Political Affairs, formulates and implements multilateral foreign policy toward the agencies of the UN.

e. The other bureaus in DOS are functionally oriented, and their assistant secretaries are responsible to other under secretaries for specific matters. These bureaus include Administration; Diplomatic Security; Consular Affairs; Human Resources; International Narcotics and Law Enforcement Affairs; Oceans and International Environmental Scientific Affairs; Political-Military Affairs; Population, Refugees, and Migration; Democracy, Human Rights, and Labor; and Economic and Business Affairs.

f. The Bureau of Political-Military Affairs (PM) is the DOS's principal link to DOD. PM provides policy direction in the areas of international security, SA, military operations, defense strategy and plans, and defense trade. PM's primary counterpart in DOD is the Office of the Assistant Secretary of Defense for International Security Affairs. Joint force planners may engage PM through the Office of the Secretary of Defense (OSD) and the Joint Staff.

g. While combatant commands are authorized to plan operations and activities directly with affected chiefs of US diplomatic missions and USAID mission directors and/or state and local authorities, they should refer all issues with DOD- or USG-level policy or resource implications through the Joint Staff to OSD for decision. Combatant command representatives who encounter these sorts of issues during routine plans coordination and information passing will not pursue them without guidance from the Office of the Under Secretary of Defense for Policy. This will ensure that the appropriate DOS bureaus are involved.

h. The chief of mission (COM), typically the ambassador, is the principal officer in charge of US diplomatic missions and US offices abroad, which the Secretary of State has designated as diplomatic in nature. As statutorily mandated, the COM directs and supervises all activities in country and coordinates the resources and programs of the USG through the country team with the exception of employees under the command of a US area military commander, and other exceptions consistent with existing statutes and authorities.

i. Joint force planners may have to wrestle with the organizational dynamics of the COM's relationship to DOS and the executive branch. The ambassador's response to a crisis will depend upon the countries in question, the crisis in question, and events in the rest of the affected region and around the world at the time. Ambassadors routinely coordinate with the assistant secretaries responsible for DOS regional bureaus. The DOS organizational structure and functional execution of foreign policy in effect constrains the ambassador's actions in many dimensions and links him or her to career foreign policy experts in Washington, DC. SFA planners should understand the operational environment and interaction between the country ambassador and the regional bureaus.

j. Conflicts between DOD and ambassador's objectives occasionally arise. The joint force planner must remember that disputes between the joint force commander (JFC) and the ambassador should be elevated to and resolved by the Secretary of State and Secretary of Defense (SecDef).

k. US Embassy Country Team. The ambassador and the deputy chief of mission (DCM) at each US embassy head the team of USG personnel, collectively known as the "country team." DOS members of the team, in addition to the ambassador and the DCM, are heads of the political, economic, administrative, consular, and security sections of the embassy. The remainder of the team encompasses the senior representatives of each of the other USG departments and agencies present at the embassy. A country team's organization is dependent on embassy size and the nature of US interests in a country, with some including over forty agencies. Each country team handles the following issues:

(1) Commercial, resource, and financial issues.

(2) Defense issues.

(3) Agricultural matters.

(4) Legal and immigration matters.

(5) Developmental and humanitarian aid matters.

l. GCC. The authority of the combatant commanders (CCDRs) is established in Chapter 6 of Title 10, USC (Title 10, USC, Sections 161-168). The Unified Command Plan establishes the missions and responsibilities for commanders of geographic combatant commands and establishes their geographic AORs. Accordingly, the GCC is the US military representative to international and US national agencies and is the single point of contact for military matters within the AOR. The GCC is responsible for planning, conducting, and assessing SC activities, and for planning and conducting military support to stability operations, humanitarian assistance, and disaster relief, as directed. Planning by a GCC is contained in TCPs. Depending on the preferences of the GCC, the TCP can be subdivided into regional campaign plans and further into country campaign plans.

m. United States Special Operations Command (USSOCOM) provides SOF in support of GCCs. SOF normally contribute to the SFA effort under operational control of the commander, theater special operations commander, or a commander, special operations component command, who has primary responsibility to plan and supervise the execution of special operations in support of the GCC or a subordinate JFC, respectively.

n. Service Component Commands. GCCs have a Service component command from each of the Services. The Service component commands provide Service-specific support and activity proposals and assist the GCC with Service-specific forces/equipment/resources that are available in the proper timeframe. Component commands also interact with parent Services or units to inform and influence training and preparation of forces to conduct specific missions. Synchronization between GCC requirements and Service component command resources is critical in meeting GCC objectives and desired end states. The Service component command also has the responsibility to ensure their Title 10, USC, role is both applicable and useful to all CCDRs.

o. In cases where the SFA/SC effort is large-scale and enduring, the GCC may establish an additional subunified command, joint task force, in a particular country or region. Examples include Combined Joint Task Force-Horn of Africa and the Combined Joint Task Force One.

CHAPTER III
PLANNING FOR SECURITY FORCE ASSISTANCE

1. Considerations for Security Force Assistance Planning

a. **TCP.** The Chairman of the Joint Chiefs of Staff directs preparation of TCPs via the Joint Strategic Capabilities Plan (JSCP), which translates broad Guidance for Employment of the Force (GEF) guidance into specific strategic and operational planning directives to CCDRs. Theater strategic end states outlined in the GEF are broad in scope and focus five to ten years into the future. For TCPs, the JSCP provides direction for developing campaign plans and expands on global defense posture, force management, and **SC matters** found in the GEF. GCCs are required to annually forecast SFA requirements to the Chairman of the Joint Chiefs of Staff and the Services to ensure those requirements can be met or to assess the risk. The TCP includes a discussion about the resources—especially forces and funding—allocated to and required by the combatant command, and addresses the impact of resource shortfalls in terms of strategic and operational risk on achievement of theater objectives. While TCPs will have a large SC-related component, they should also address posture, ongoing combat operations, where applicable, and the phase 0 component of the combatant command's contingency planning or generally setting the theater. Theater campaign planning should incorporate country planning, and the GCC's country plans or in some cases regional plans, should align with the COM's goals because TCP activities and resource investments typically occur at the country level. Senior defense officials/defense attachés (SDOs/DATTs), supported by the combatant commands' SC offices, help coordinate and align country planning with COM goals. Individual country plans should add further details regarding the routine SC activities that would include SFA activities.

b. **Country Plan.** Country plans, or country campaign plans in some TCPs, should be developed concurrently with the TCP, and may be made part of it. They should discuss the country objectives and the role the USG expects the country to play in achieving theater objectives. A country plan provides guidance to various DOD elements who implement and support planned SC activities. These elements include the geographic and functional combatant commands, Service components, and SDOs/DATTs.

(1) **Scope.** Country plans provide the roadmap of specific engagement activities that a GCC intends to conduct over one to three years. These activities include day-to-day presence missions, military-to-military exchanges, and combined exercises. The plan should provide guidance to Service components and other DOD planners and inform and be informed by both the COM's integrated country strategy, and, if applicable, USAID country development strategy. Reviewing a country plan with the HN as the TCP is developed facilitates alignment of US and HN goals.

(2) **SFA Activities.** Subordinate unified commands and Service component commands prepare supporting plans to the GCC's TCP. Depending on the GCC, these supporting plans may include a wrap-up of country-specific support to GCC country plans, or separate supporting plans developed for each country plan. Regardless, the Service components are responsible for developing the Service-specific SFA proposals that meet the vision in the program of activities and milestones of the country plans. The GCC performs a

detailed review of each proposed activity to identify the appropriate authority or authorities that enable that activity. Each identified authority is reviewed for adequate levels of funding, as well as consideration of the timeline required to process the activity under the identified authority.

c. The initial theater assessment, "where we are today," is the baseline of the TCP, and should provide an overview of the current theater security environment and relevant strategic trends, both positive and negative, to include key partners, critical partners, and other actors of concern. A mission statement and concept of engagement provide the operational approaches and actions needed to achieve theater objectives and describe the priorities for theater shaping, force posture and access, building partnership capacity, and routine operations support. Intermediate military objectives, the milestones that must be met over time to reach the strategic end state, are identified, and lines of efforts may be introduced. Coordinating instructions address plan design and execution to include authorities, key enabling agreements, operational limitations, assumptions, and strategic communication themes—all of which provide context on how objectives will be achieved.

d. Development of plans that include SFA activities should include specific and measurable objectives and assessment criteria. Since the purpose of SFA is to build capability and capacity within FSF and their supporting institutions, the plan should clearly state what capability the HN's security force requires at a future time horizon. The recommended time horizon for these capability and capacity end states will vary and may be five years or greater to align with resource planning. Desired capabilities should include appropriate measures of performance (MOP) and measures of effectiveness (MOE). For example, if a country requires a riverine force able to patrol and control illicit shipping traffic along 200 miles of a certain river continuously, twenty-four hours a day, in limited visibility, and in all weather conditions. This specific capability statement enables assessments against measurable objectives. The country plan should include an assessment of the HN's current capability to achieve the specific desired capability end state related to SFA activities. Results of inspections, visits, examinations, tests, or exercises may all contribute to this assessment. Due to a variety of factors, this assessment may be limited to subjective inputs from US Armed Forces members familiar with the HN, such as the SDO/DATT, or allied counterparts. Related to the above riverine example, a current assessment of the patrol may state its current capability as limited to no more than 50 miles of river for a maximum of 30 days before ceasing all operations for refit and maintenance.

For further information on TCPs and country plans, refer to DOD Theater Campaign Planning; Planners Handbook.

2. Security Force Assistance Goals

a. The ultimate goal of SFA activities is to create FSF that are competent, capable, sustainable, committed, and confident, and have a security apparatus tied to regional stability. Regional security may partly be achieved in partnership with an HN by developing its ability to deter and defend against military aggression by its neighbors and to combat lawlessness, subversion, insurgency, and terrorist threats.

b. SFA activities should improve FSF to become competent, capable and sustainable, committed, and confident:

(1) Competent

(a) Across all levels, ministerial to the individual soldier or police officer, or other individuals performing security functions.

(b) Across all functions (operational, enabling, sustaining, and institutional).

(2) Capable and Sustainable

(a) Appropriately sized and effective enough to accomplish missions.

(b) Sustainable over time.

(c) Resourced within HN capabilities.

(3) Committed

(a) To survival of the state and security for all its people.

(b) To preservation of the liberties and human rights of the citizens.

(c) To peaceful transition of power.

(4) Confident

(a) In themselves and their ability to secure the country.

(b) The citizens trust the FSF will provide security, respond to crises, remain professional, and conduct their responsibilities within the rule of law.

(c) The HN government is confident they have the appropriate type and amount of FSF.

(d) The international community supports the FSF.

(5) Accountable

(a) For their use of power within a framework of rule of law.

(b) The citizens trust the FSF will provide security, respond to crises, and remain professional and accountable.

3. Imperatives

The following imperatives are essential to SFA activities, and they have universal application for the numerous SC activities and larger-scale Service/joint operations and missions supported by SFA activities.

a. **Understand the Operational Environment.** Understanding the operational environment is fundamental to joint operations and critical to SFA activities. An in-depth understanding of the operational environment includes the size, organization, capabilities, disposition, roles, functions, and mission focus of HN forces, opposing threats, and especially the sociocultural factors of the indigenous and other relevant populations. Identifying all actors influencing the environment and their motivations will help planners and practitioners define the goals and methods for developing HN security forces and their institutions. To prioritize and focus the SFA effort, it is equally important to understand the regional players and transnational actors who may influence the **security environment.** The basis for a holistic view and understanding of the operational environment are products of the joint intelligence preparation of the operational environment process, integrated with the separate intelligence preparation of the battlespace products of the component commands and Service intelligence centers. Joint/Service planners can employ a number of processes and tools to evaluate environmental factors such as areas, structures, capabilities, organizations, people and events, and political, military, economic, social, information, and infrastructure.

See JP 2-03.1, Joint Intelligence Preparation of the Operational Environment, *for additional details.*

b. **Ensure Unity of Effort.** The SFA effort may include multinational partners or an IGO. Effective command organizational and stakeholder relationships warrant special consideration. Unity of command is typically preferable, but often impractical. Unity of effort is imperative to successful SFA efforts. Command relationships and organizational relationship agreements may range from simple to complex and military commanders may answer to nonmilitary personnel such as a COM. Regardless of the relationship, clear delineation and understanding of authorities is essential to avoid confusion. Additionally, establishing coordinating boards or centers assists unity of effort among US and multinational partners.

c. **Provide Effective Leadership.** Depending on the circumstances, the US may execute an SFA mission unilaterally, or as part of a multinational force. In any case, leadership is especially important in the inherently dynamic and complex environment associated with SFA. SFA normally requires the personal interaction of trainers/advisors and trainees, military and civilians, from the tactical level to the strategic level, so a high premium is placed on effective leadership at all levels, from the most junior noncommissioned officer to the most senior general or flag officer or civilian official. Leadership must fully comprehend the operational environment and be prepared, engaged, and supportive for SFA activities to succeed. Productive SFA requires leadership on both the provider and the recipient sides throughout the operation or campaign.

d. **Build Legitimacy.** SFA develops FSF that contribute to the legitimate governance of the HN population. This is done by developing FSF that are competent, capable, committed, and confident, not only in the eyes of the US, other countries, and HN governments, but more critically, in the eyes of the HN population. Creating the effect of legitimacy is critical to the objectives of SFA. Leaders, planners, and practitioners at all levels who integrate SFA activities into SC planning efforts must consider how each action may affect popular perceptions, and focus activities that enable the legitimacy of the HN government and FSF, not just make them technically competent. While it is important to assist HN forces to develop professionally, a mirror image US model may not be the optimum solution for some FSF, because of sociocultural factors. Legitimacy may be very tenuous during a complex insurgency, and may be difficult to measure objectively.

e. **Synchronized Information.** Information is a powerful enabler in the complex and dynamic environment typical of SFA activities and requires synchronization between SFA and the overarching operation or campaign (e.g., FID, COIN, or stability operation). Advisors must work with the FSF to develop themes and messages that give positive context and narrative to the FSF's professionalization efforts and capacity to secure the population. Synchronized information between the US, FSF, the HN government, and the population can limit or mitigate the propaganda efforts of insurgents or hostile forces. This sets the conditions for success and may serve to mitigate the potential for destabilizing influences of hostile forces or criminal elements to propagandize SFA efforts and damage the HN government's credibility and legitimacy.

f. **Sustainability.** Providing sustainability consists of two major components: the ability of the US and other partners to sustain the SFA activities successfully through all phases of the operation or campaign, and the ability of HN security forces to sustain their capabilities independently over the long term. The first component may be predicated on the PN maintaining legitimacy while the second component should be considered holistically when working with the HN to build their security forces. It is important to consider the sociocultural factors, infrastructure, and education levels of prospective FSF when fielding weapons systems and maintaining organizations.

g. **Support HN Ownership.** The HN's history, culture, legal framework, and institutions must inform the principles, policies, laws, and structures that form an SFA program. As a result, the needs, priorities, and circumstances driving SFA will differ substantially from one country to another. Accounting for the basic security concerns of the HN population is essential for attaining buy-in and is essential to the success of SFA. To ensure the sustainability of reforms, assistance should be designed to meet the needs of the HN population and to support HN agencies, processes, and priorities. To accomplish this, SFA generally should be developed to serve longer-term goals.

h. **Incorporate Principles of Good Governance and Respect for Human Rights.** Accountability, transparency, public participation, respect for human rights, and legitimacy must be mainstreamed in security force development. Military and civilian security forces must carry out their core functions in accordance with these principles. This is particularly important in rebuilding countries where the legacy of abuse by security personnel may have eroded public confidence in the sector overall. SFA programs should include accountability and oversight mechanisms, including thorough direct collaboration with civil society, to prevent abuses of power and corruption, and to build public confidence. Vetting is routinely done prior to giving provisional assistance or training to security forces. Likewise, SFA programs must incorporate an explicit focus on security sector governance. Strengthening the overall legal, policy, and budgetary frameworks should be an important component of SFA into any country.

i. **Link Security and Justice.** A country's security policies and practices must be founded upon the rule of law and linked to the broader justice sector. SFA should aim to ensure that all security forces operate within the bounds of domestic and international law, and that they support wide-ranging efforts to enforce and promote the rule of law. The police in particular should operate as an integral part of the justice system and directly support other parts of the justice sector, including the courts and corrections institutions. Assistance to the police and other state security providers may need to be complemented with other efforts to strengthen these institutions, to avoid unintended consequences, and to ensure that the security forces operate according to the law. Experience demonstrates, for example, that police assistance undertaken absent efforts to strengthen other parts of the justice system can lead to increased arrests without the necessary means to adjudicate cases, or defend, incarcerate, or rehabilitate suspected offenders. In addition, although the tendency may be to focus on criminal justice systems, civil justice reform may have important implications for law and order, particularly with respect to the resolution of potential conflict drivers, such as land disputes.

j. **Foster Transparency.** Effective SFA programs should be conducted transparently and openly whenever possible. Program design should include a robust Service component command to foster awareness of reform efforts among HN officials and the population, neighboring countries, the donor community, and others with a potential stake in program outcomes. Likewise, DOS, DOD, and USAID practitioners should engage in broad consultation with other USG agencies, nongovernmental organizations (NGOs), IGOs, international donors, and the media, to enhance program development and program execution.

k. **Do No Harm.** In complex environments, donor assistance can become a part of the conflict dynamic serving either to increase or reduce tension. As with any activity that involves changes to the status quo, SSR planners and implementers must pay close attention to minimize adverse effects on the local population and community structures, the security sector, or the wider political, social, and economic climate in unanticipated or unintended ways. Developing a thorough understanding of the system for which change is sought, and the actual needs that exist, is a prerequisite for the success of any SFA-related activity. Practitioners should conduct a risk assessment prior to implementation and be prepared to adjust activities over the lifetime of the SFA program.

4. **Security Force Functions**

a. Security forces perform three generic functions: executive, generating, and operating. The executive function includes strategic direction that provides oversight, policy, and resources for the FSF generating and operating functions. FSF generating forces refer to the capability and capacity of the FSF to organize, train, equip, and build operating force units.

FSF operating forces form operational capabilities through the use of concepts similar to the US joint functions to achieve FSF security objectives. Of note, specific generating and operating forces may have some overlap of requirements and responsibilities. In some FSF, a single organization may perform all three functions.

b. The SFA planner requires knowledge of how his own organization distributes these functions as well as how the FSF implement them in their system in order to identify the SFA tasks that will support the FSF's model rather than simply importing a US model to the FSF organization. Figure III-1 shows the primary duties of each function and identifies the relationship of the OTERA tasks.

c. **Executive Function.** All security forces apply some level of executive function which empowers the generating and operating functions. The entities that perform this function direct and develop national policy and resources for their security forces. The executive organization justifies, authorizes, and directs parameters for the generating and operating forces. The OSD, the Joint Staff, and the Service staffs perform this function for the US. The duties associated with the executive function are:

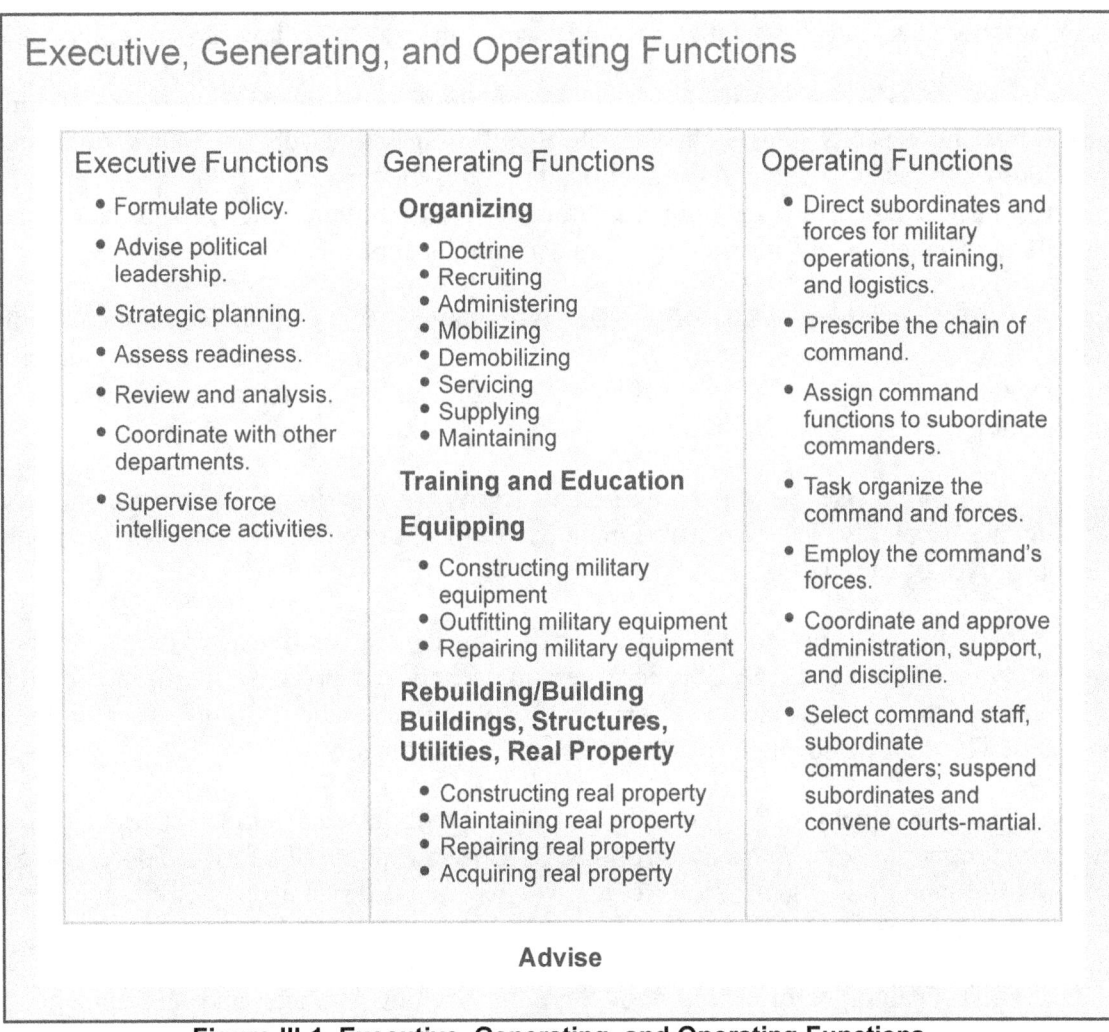

Figure III-1. Executive, Generating, and Operating Functions

(1) **Formulate Policy.** The executive organization establishes the regulation of SFA in the context of the political purpose that department, agency, organization, Service, or unit serves. This includes forecasting and budgeting for current and future requirements in both the operating and generating functions and requests or allocating resources to meet the anticipated priorities.

(2) **Advise Political Leadership.** The executive organization provides an understanding of problems and solutions in relation to security force issues. These may include, but are not limited to, force employment options, operational requirements, or military and political consequences of pending decisions.

(3) **Strategic Planning.** The executive supports formulation of security force plans to achieve a desired political end. Strategic planning encompasses not only the delivery and employment of operational forces, but also considers the required capabilities which should be generated and sustained to achieve those ends, as well as the associated second and third order effects.

(4) **Assess Readiness.** The executive organization identifies capability or capacity gaps as they relate to the functions, roles, and missions which security force departments, agencies, Services, and organizations should perform in order to achieve a political purpose.

(5) **Review and Analysis.** The executive provides insights into current or future capability and capacity gaps as they relate to fulfilling known or anticipated roles and missions for the security force. As a function, it requires the capability to collect and process relative information from operations, exercises, or experiments and then package and distribute the analysis in a manner useful to decision makers.

(6) **Coordinate with Other Departments.** The executive coordinates with departments, agencies, ministries and organizations that are external to the security organization to ensure effective, efficient, economical administration and to reduce duplication.

(7) **Supervise Force Intelligence Activities.** Military organizations have intelligence capability. The executive function controls these efforts to ensure they support the objectives of national security.

d. **Generating Function.** The generating function develops and sustains the capabilities of the operating forces. In the US, the generating function is primarily performed by the Services. For the US, this function is performed by its military schools, training centers, and arsenals. The duties associated with the generating function are:

(1) **Organizing.** Supports recruiting, mobilization/demobilization, force management, resourcing, distribution, or other efforts that support the forming or reforming of units and supporting organizations required to generate and sustain capabilities that meet operational requirements.

(2) **Training and Education.** Supports the development and sustainment of systems that provide the resources (doctrine, materiel, funds, terrain, time, personnel,

regulations) required to identify, achieve, and sustain a level of training readiness to meet operational requirements.

(3) **Equipping.** Develops, tests, fields, distributes, and maintains the materiel required for security force personnel and organizations to train and execute those tasks associated with their roles and missions.

(4) **Rebuilding/Building.** Develops and maintains the physical infrastructure required to generate forces. This may include installations, ranges, buildings, road networks, airfields, shipyards, or other security force related infrastructure.

e. **Operating Function.** The operating function employs military capabilities through application of joint functions of maneuver, intelligence, fires, force protection, sustainment, and command and control during actual operations. Operating, as it applies to police security forces, may include training and actual operations with the integration of patrolling, forensics, apprehension, intelligence, investigations, incarceration, communications, and sustainment. Operating forces are responsible for collective training and performing missions assigned to the unit. In the US, operating forces are normally employed by the CCDRs to achieve US security objectives.

(1) US operating forces are typically better suited to develop FSF operating forces or operational capabilities than they are to developing FSF generating forces of generating capabilities. Typically, they are tasked to train and/or advise FSF operating forces.

(2) Employing operational forces to fill SFA capabilities associated with developing the FSF's generating function (FSF tasks such as "develop FSF doctrine" or "stand up a staff officer's college"), and possibly in the FSF's executive function (e.g., ministries) would likely be beyond the inherent capability of the operating force and would likely require special training or augmentation by subject matter experts drawn from US generating organizations.

5. **Foreign Security Force Development Tasks**

SFA activities normally use the tasks of OTERA to develop the functional capabilities required by the FSF. OTERA tasks are a tool to develop, change, or improve the capability and capacity of FSF. Through a baseline assessment of the subject FSF, and considering US interests and objectives, planners can determine which OTERA tasks will be required to build the proper capability and capacity levels within the various units of the FSF. Assessments of the FSF against a desired set of capabilities will assist in developing an OTERA-based plan to improve FSF. The following are basic descriptions of the OTERA tasks.

a. **Organize.** All activities taken to create, improve, and integrate doctrinal principles, organizational structures, capability constructs, and personnel management. This may include doctrine development, unit or organization design, command and staff processes, and recruiting and manning functions.

b. **Train.** All activities taken to create, improve, and integrate training, leader development, and education at the individual, leader, collective, and staff levels. This may include task analysis, the development and execution of programs of instruction, implementation of training events, and leader development activities.

c. **Equip.** All activities to design, improve, and integrate materiel and equipment, procurement, fielding, accountability, and maintenance through life cycle management. This may also include fielding of new equipment, operational readiness processes, repair, and recapitalization.

d. **Rebuild or Build.** All activities to create, improve, and integrate facilities. This may include physical infrastructures such as bases and stations, lines of communication, ranges and training complexes, and administrative structures.

e. **Advise/Assist.** All activities to provide subject matter expertise, guidance, advice, and counsel to FSF while carrying out the missions assigned to the unit or organization. Advising may occur under combat or administrative conditions, at tactical through strategic levels, and in support of individuals or groups.

6. General Theater Planning Considerations

a. **General.** DOD maintains capabilities for SFA activities to train FSF and build supporting HN institutions across the range of military operations. Conducting SFA activities in the midst of an insurgency or major combat operations has proven a difficult challenge for US forces and interagency and other partners. The inherent cultural, political, leadership, and other complexities associated with any SFA mission demand careful and deliberate attention from planners. SFA activities should be a critical part of the strategic and operational planning from the beginning, including the GCC's theater strategy and theater campaign and contingency planning to support GCC's strategic objectives. SFA should be integrated into the specific operation or campaign plans in all phases, not just as an afterthought for the stabilize and enable civil authority phases following combat operations. Early planning should involve joint and interagency partners, whenever possible, to marshal and focus US capabilities and maximize capabilities of the HN and its allies. Military oversight and administration of SFA activities during phases 0, I, and V is normally conducted by an office of SC, an office of defense cooperation, or an SA office. Military oversight and administration of SFA activities during phases II, III, and IV is typically conducted by the joint forces commander or his designated representative.

(1) **Phases 0 (Shaping) and I (Deter).** Execution of relevant SFA activities in phases 0 and I builds an HN organic capability designed to manage destabilizing events. Numerous SC activities, including SFA, are conducted during the phase 0 of GCCs' TCPs around the globe. It also provides an existing, effective HN security force that US and multinational forces may partner with in the event outside intervention is required to reestablish stability.

(2) **Phases II (Seize Initiative) and III (Dominate).** Execution of relevant SFA activities in phases II and III provides the HN the support needed to assure friendly freedom

of action and access to theater infrastructure, and ensures the HN establishes dominant capabilities, with or without US combat operations, and achieves conditions for transition to phase IV.

(3) **Phase IV (Stabilize).** Execution of relevant SFA activities in phase IV supports the establishment of security by preparing the HN to assume full responsibility for internal and external security during the transfer to civil authorities and redeployment of US and multinational forces. Phase IV SFA activities generally focus on building essential capabilities and capacities in HN's security force for transition to phase V.

(4) **Phase V (Enable Civil Authorities).** In phase V the HN government is conducting security operations with minimal direct US assistance and continues to work with the US through normal DOS and DOD channels to access US SA programs.

b. **Methodology: Ends, Ways, Means.** Successful strategies typically employ all USG instruments of national power. Ends are the desired strategic outcomes or end states. Ways are the methods, tactics, and procedures used to achieve the ends. Means are the resources required to achieve the ends, such as troops, weapons systems, money, will, and time. All strategies are subject to risk, often associated with the means allocated against a particular way. The ends must be reasonable given the means and ways available. Figure III-2 depicts a model for SFA activities.

7. Security Force Assistance Assessment

a. **FSF Assessment Coordination.** Assessment of the FSF and its functional components should precede development in order to determine FSF capability gaps. Appropriate subject matter experts should assess FSF capabilities and capacity based on the USG anticipated end state. From the baseline, assessment continues throughout FSF development to measure the effectiveness of SFA efforts and levels of FSF developmental efforts. FSF organizational assessments should categorize which organizations fulfill FSF executive direction, generating force, or operating force roles and functions. It is important to assess these organizations in relation to one another and to some agreed upon standards. The MOE for the generating forces is how well the operating forces perform their assigned tasks. In order for the generating force to serve its purpose, the operating forces should communicate their requirements back to the generating forces. Assessments should include all FSF generating and operating functions in relation to the executive direction function; each provides insight as to the will and capability of the FSF to generate, employ, and sustain itself.

b. Each echelon should conduct assessments. The GCC initially conducts strategic assessments in coordination with the country team to determine what overarching gaps in capability or capacity need to be addressed within the context of US country and regional interests, objectives, and goals. This strategic assessment forms the basis for the SFA plan and for future, more detailed assessments at the ministerial, operational, and tactical levels. This process helps frame proper SFA activities within the larger context of SC supporting US strategic interests.

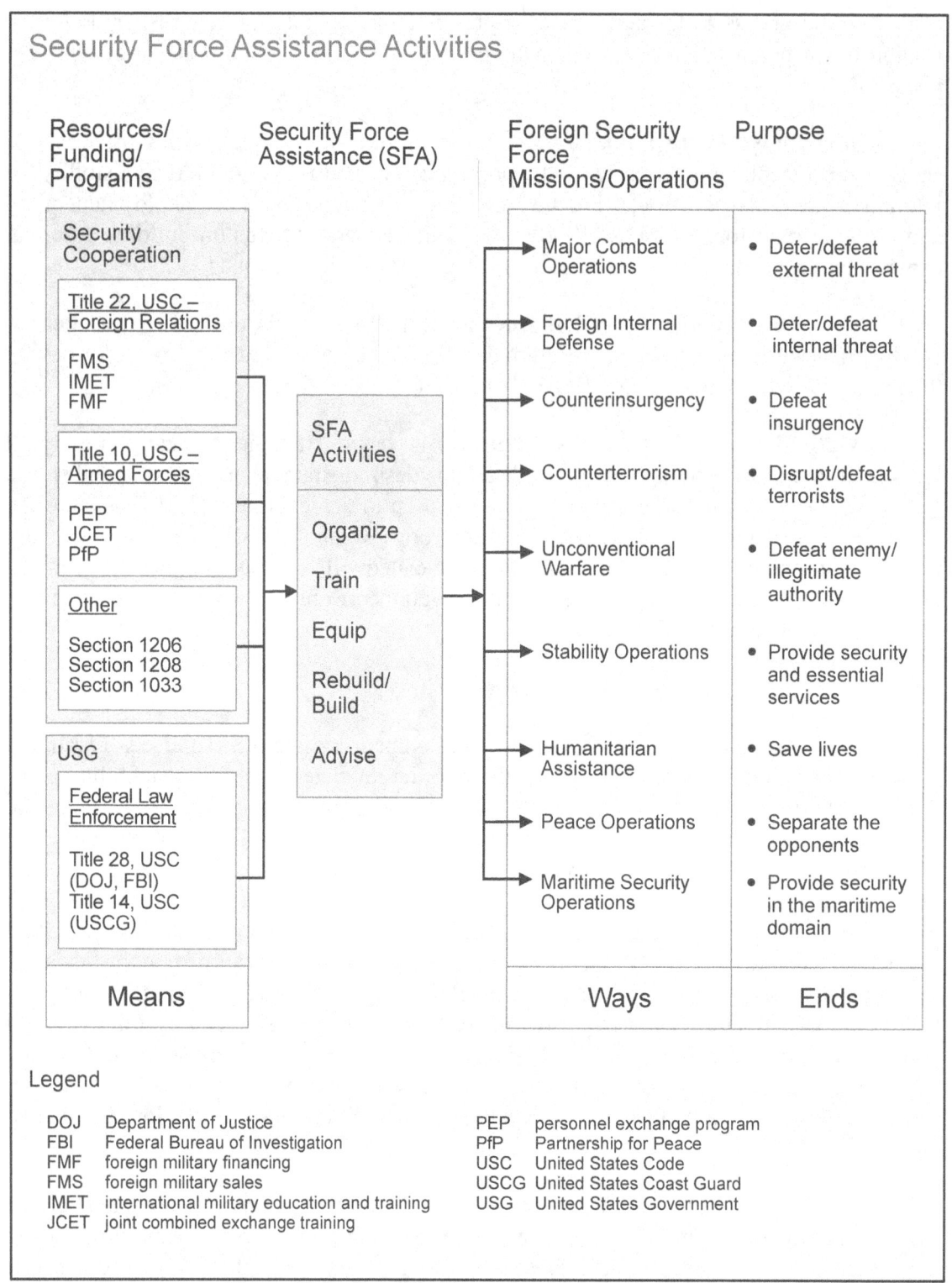

Figure III-2. Security Force Assistance Activities

c. **FSF Assessment Workflow.** Before assessing FSF, it is important to understand FSF requirements. This assessment of requirements applies at all echelons. For example, an independent light infantry company will have different requirements than one belonging to an airborne infantry battalion. Following an understanding of requirements, the FSF assessment takes place in terms of the tasks required of the FSF, the conditions the FSF will operate under, and the minimum standards required for achieving successful outcomes.

d. The FSF assessment enables the SFA organization to establish the correct developmental objectives. Individual unit specific FSF assessments of individual FSF units allow for effective alignment of feasible developmental tasks. The comprehensive FSF assessment provides a thorough understanding of the FSF and presents a baseline in FSF capability requirements within the context of the operational environment. The FSF assessment task workflow consists of five steps (see Figure III-3).

e. Continuous assessment of MOPs and MOEs provides measurable feedback in the developmental progress for a specific FSF unit and collectively across the FSF. It answers not only **what, but how well** an FSF is currently doing. Assessment also identifies what tasks the FSF must perform and to what standard through MOPs, along with MOEs that may highlight factors impeding or enabling the FSF in accomplishing its developmental objectives.

f. Planners and advisors can apply this FSF assessment process as a primary developmental tool in day-to-day activities as well as broader program development to synchronize development objectives of FSF generating and operating forces. Finally, when standardized among SFA organizations, the FSF assessment workflow provides a collective understanding of trends and progress across the FSF.

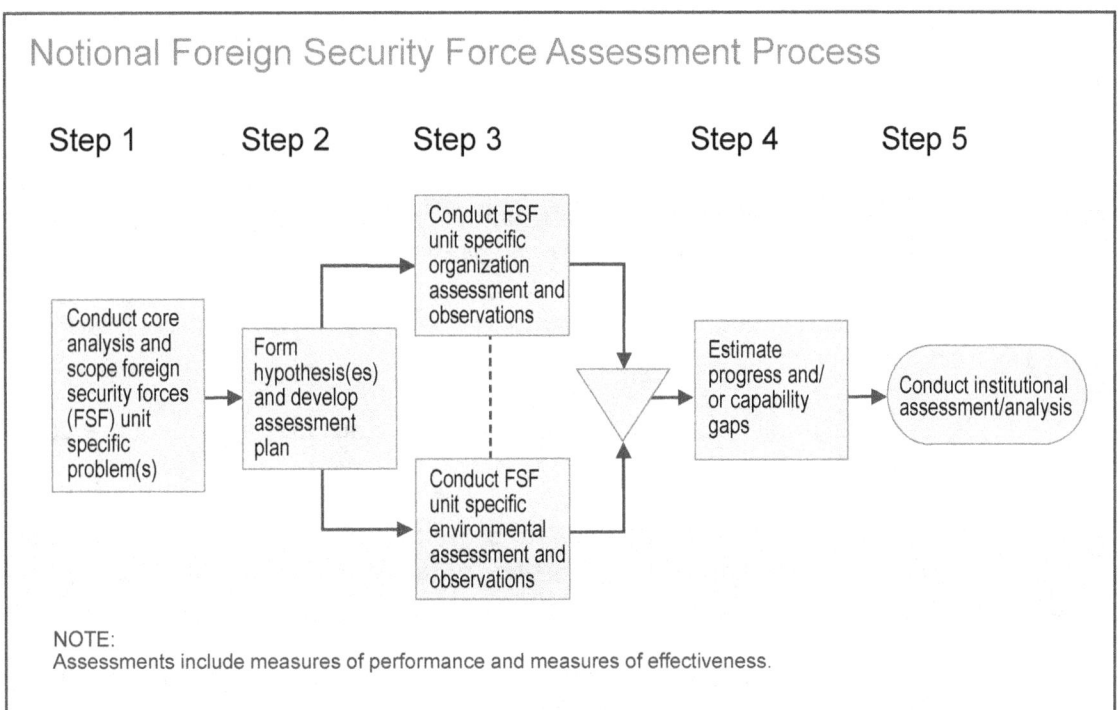

Figure III-3. Notional Foreign Security Force Assessment Process

See JP 5-0, Joint Operation Planning, *for additional details regarding assessments, including use of MOPs and MOEs.*

g. The initial site assessment refines information or mission parameters developed during previous assessments in the planning process. Site survey and assessment teams should include a counterintelligence representative, a strategic planner, a force protection element, and a foreign area officer. Units tasked to perform SFA activities should determine or identify:

(1) The HN unit mission and its equivalent mission-essential task list and its capability to execute them.

(2) The organizational tables for authorized personnel and equipment and for personnel and equipment actually on hand.

(3) Any past or present foreign military presence or influence in doctrine, training, or combat operations.

(4) The unit's ability to retain and support acquired skills or training from past mobile training teams (MTTs) or foreign training missions.

(5) The organization and leadership level that is responsible for training the individual security force personnel. Does the HN have institutional training established? Is it effective?

(6) Any operational deficiencies during recent combat operations or participation in joint or multinational exercises with US personnel.

(7) The status of maintenance for major end items, to include maintenance training programs.

(8) The language or languages in which SFA activities will take place.

(9) The religious, tribal, or other affiliations within the HN forces (notably the differences between HN forces and the local populace).

(10) The potential security concerns with employing US Armed Forces (and allies) in the HN operational area.

(11) The local infrastructure and possible positive or negative impacts of operations on the local populace.

(12) The local populace's attitudes toward US Armed Forces and government personnel, as well as ordinary US citizens (to include presence and behavior of expatriate US populations).

(13) The local populace's sociocultural factors, especially their prejudices or fears.

(14) Potential emergency egress routes for friendly forces and designated safe areas or potential sanctuaries.

(15) Force protection concerns, personnel recovery considerations, and potential mitigation measures.

(16) Any key local leaders, communicators, and potential spoilers.

(17) The presence, agendas, capabilities, influence, and attitudes of NGOs and IGOs.

Intentionally Blank

CHAPTER IV
SECURITY FORCE ASSISTANCE ACTIVITIES

1. General

a. Discussion of SFA in the previous chapters has generally centered on strategic and operational levels. This chapter transitions to a more focused examination of employment principles, techniques, and procedures used in conducting SFA activities.

b. **SFA activities are part of the unified actions of the GCC and require interagency coordination.** Even small tactical operations usually require interagency coordination, most often through the SC office during phases 0 (shaping), I (deter), and V (enable civil authorities), and through a joint/multinational force or Service component headquarters organization during phases II (seize initiative), III (dominate), and IV (stabilize) that are normally part of a contingency operation/campaign.

c. Interagency coordination for SC such as SFA activities is normally led by the COM and coordinated through the country team. In the complete absence of a COM, which is very rare and only likely due to extremely severe security problems, the senior USG official may be the JFC who would lead the interagency coordination of USG participants, and if required, interorganizational coordination for all participants involved in the operation/campaign. **Civilian military teaming** is a product of interagency coordination, and good examples are the provincial reconstruction teams used in Iraq and Afghanistan. The strategic and operational level coordination results in planning and resources for effective tactical level application. SFA activities may be conducted with FSF through large joint/Service task forces as well as through smaller civilian military teams.

2. Employment Factors

As in planning, several areas deserve special attention when discussing employment of forces in SFA activities.

a. **Information Operations (IO) Impact.** IO are the integrated employment, during military operations, of information-related capabilities in concert with other lines of operation to influence, disrupt, corrupt, or usurp the decision making of adversaries and potential adversaries while protecting our own. IO employs information-related capabilities to affect the perceptions and attitudes of adversaries, the HN population, and the international community. The integration of information-related capabilities in all aspects of planning and execution is important when conducting SFA activities. An SFA representative should be part of the IO cell.

b. **Psychological Impact.** Considering the psychological impact of SFA activities on the FSF, the HN populace, and the joint force is important regardless of where or when it takes place. The effects may occur collaterally as a result of another operation, or directly as a result of an operation specifically executed for its psychological effect.

c. **Intelligence Support.** Intelligence provides an assessment of HN and potential adversaries' capabilities, capacities, and shortfalls. It involves understanding sociocultural factors, information and intelligence sharing, and intelligence training. Information sharing between US and HN must be an early consideration for planners. This continuous intelligence effort will gauge the reaction of the local populace and determine the effects on the infrastructure of US efforts as well as evaluate strengths, weaknesses, and disposition of opposition groups in the area. Ultimately, intelligence supports the US and HN leaders decision-making processes, and supports the protection of friendly forces and assets.

d. **Force Selection.** US forces have some inherent ability to assess, train, advise, and assist foreign forces. The degree to which they can be tasked depends on their preparation in terms of cultural knowledge, language, functional skills, and the ability to apply these skills within the operational environment. Employing operational designs that provide a combination of CF while leveraging the unique capabilities of SOF will assist in achieving objectives. The planning for and selection of the appropriate mix of CF, SOF, CEW, and/or civilian personnel and contractors should be a deliberate decision based on thorough mission analysis and a pairing of available capabilities to requirements. Important factors to consider in these decisions include the nature of the HN force, the nature of the skills or competencies required by the HN force, and the nature of the situation and environment into which US forces will deploy.

(1) **SOF.** SOF may conduct SFA activities independently in the absence of any other military effort, support other ongoing military or civilian assistance efforts, or support the employment of CF. Many SOF units are theater or regionally oriented through language training, sociocultural awareness, military engagement, and positive training experiences with FSF in countries in the theater.

(a) In addition to the specific capability requirements that may call for the selection of SOF, the nature of the SFA mission may dictate the use of SOF. SOF's unique capabilities for language, cultural awareness, and regional focus may be required when the environment involves particular political sensitivities. Additionally, SOF's ability to conduct short-notice missions with only modest support makes them adept at initiating programs for hand-over to CF.

(b) USSOCOM provides SOF in support of GCCs. SOF normally contribute to the SFA effort under operational control of the theater special operations commander, who has primary responsibility to plan and supervise the execution of SOF operations in support of the GCC. SOF also may provide dedicated theater forces. When planning for use of SOF, it is important to assess command and control requirements among the combatant command, the country team, and SOF. Communications requirements, administration, logistics, and contingency considerations should also be clearly stated.

(2) **CF.** When the mission requires broader action to support HN security capability and capacity development efforts, the JFC may employ CF for SFA activities. This may include serving as military advisors, conducting MTTs, embedding or partnering US personnel and units with HN units, conducting joint and multinational exercises with HN units, and assisting in the development of supporting institutions. CF units and personnel

may also be more appropriate in SFA activities focused on higher echelon organizations (e.g., divisions, corps, and wings) or on Service or ministerial-level efforts. Commanders should provide subordinates with clear guidance to prepare their forces to conduct SFA.

(3) Use of civilians/contractors with a specialized niche capability unique to SFA.

(a) United States Coast Guard (USCG) training teams, personnel, and platforms are well suited to support the development of stable, multi-mission maritime forces to respond to many transnational threats. USCG SFA activities reach beyond normal military-to-military relations to a broader HN maritime audience, including, but not limited to, law enforcement agencies, maritime administrations, and transport ministries.

(b) National Guard State Partnership Program. The National Guard's State Partnership Program establishes partnerships between foreign countries and US states and is an important contribution to the DOD's SC programs conducted by the CCDRs and US COM programs implemented outside of DOD. It provides unique, niche capabilities in direct support to the GCCs and COM in meeting their theater and country engagement objectives as authorized under Title 10, USC, and Title 22, USC, respectively.

e. **Operational Environment and Employment Tasking of SFA Forces.** A key element of planning and employment of forces addresses the environment in which DOD is directed to conduct SFA activities. Regardless of the operational context, there are three potential conditions that GCC's planners should consider when integrating SFA activities into strategy and plans. These criteria assist in determining the optimal integration of force capabilities and the proper combinations of SOF, CF, CEW personnel, and contractors.

(1) **Politically sensitive environments where an overt US presence is unacceptable to the host-country government.** Note: Discussion of overt presence here means large, visible US presence. This does not mean that a covert presence is acceptable or will be utilized. This environment traditionally lends itself to a primarily SOF solution. The GCC's planners should assess the specific skills and competencies required to accomplish the mission, and tailor the force using the appropriate combination of personnel and contractors.

(2) **Environments where a limited, overt US presence is acceptable to the HN government.** This condition lends itself to either a SOF-led or a CF-led combination, based upon the capabilities required and the purpose of the operation. A small to mid-sized team or element composed of a mix of SOF, CF, CEW personnel and contractor capabilities may be optimum. The balance of US capabilities required, signature, and duration of the activity, as well as the availability of US resources should be considered to arrive at the most effective operational and strategic solution.

(3) **Environments where a large-scale US presence is considered necessary and acceptable by the HN government.** In this case, the apparent solution may be CF-led, principally CF-manned activity, with SOF integrated to accomplish specific SOF tasks or engage with SOF HN elements. The GCC's planners should direct their assessments toward those capabilities and functions that are, or may be, CF- or SOF-specific, and consider the

target HN elements engaged, to develop options for the integration of forces. The primary considerations are the HN requirements, HN elements to be engaged, CF- or SOF-unique skills and competencies required, and the strategic priorities driven by the theater commander.

f. **Public Information.** Public information is key during all phases of any mission with SFA activities. While it is important to support the USG effort through information-related capabilities such as military information support operations (MISO), it is also important to employ effective public affairs (PA) program to inform the US and HN populations of current SFA activities, goals, and objectives. Without popular HN support it may be impractical to fully develop and sustain missions that require USG support for FSF. At the US national level, public diplomacy activities will accurately communicate US efforts to foreign audiences and opinion makers. The President or SecDef also support this national program through the GCC's or subordinate JFC's PA activities designed to disclose the maximum amount of information possible within PA guidelines and applicable security restrictions. Coordination is important between the PA staff and the media, the country team, the MISO unit, and other information agencies within the HN and region.

g. **Logistics Support.** Logistics support of SFA activities might include support of both US and HN forces for their primary operational missions (e.g., supporting HN civilians or military forces with medical, construction, maintenance, supply, or transportation capabilities). There are several general guidelines for logistic issues in support of US forces conducting SFA activities.

(1) There may be a ceiling imposed on the number of US military personnel authorized in the HN to conduct SFA activities. Commanders should determine how external or sea-basing of some forces affects that situation. Maximum use should be made of host-nation support (HNS) capabilities, but where reliance on the HN is not feasible, minimizing logistic support requirements is essential. SFA and supporting activities may include contractor personnel, which could complicate legal, diplomatic, administrative, budgetary, and logistical issues. Efficient use of throughput of supplies (an average quantity that can pass through a port on a daily basis), airlift resupply, and inter-Service support agreements should also be considered.

(2) Commanders should carefully balance the advantages of using HNS with the risks of establishing dependency on potentially unreliable sources.

(3) The type of mission determines logistics operations. Integrated into the overall joint force are the Services' logistics support elements. Logistics support for deployed forces, however, remains a Service responsibility.

(4) Other multinational forces supporting the SFA mission often require support beyond their organic capabilities. Accordingly, when conducting SFA with multinational partners, there becomes a need to establish multinational logistic support agreements. Identifying the need for such nonorganic support should occur during the planning phase and be arranged for prior to beginning SFA activities. Acquisition and cross-servicing agreements negotiated with multinational partners are beneficial as they allow US forces to

exchange most common types of support. SecDef typically delegates authority to negotiate these agreements to the supported GCC.

For further information on international logistics, refer to JP 4-08, Logistics in Support of Multinational Operations.

h. Force Protection

(1) It is incumbent upon the commander to fully understand the threat environment in the operational area. By having access to fused intelligence from local, regional and national resources, commanders can accurately assess threats and employ measures to safeguard SFA personnel and facilities. Force protection planning considerations should address additional support requirements for quick reaction forces, emergency procedures, personnel recovery, or the requirement to integrate SFA personnel into the HN protection plan.

(2) Insider attacks are a real threat in any operational area. Commanders should ensure that personnel are trained to identify behavioral indicators of possible insider threats and the means to apply prevention tools to mitigate this threat. Cultural awareness yields situational awareness and leads to increased force protection for SFA personnel.

i. **Operations Security (OPSEC).** A significant challenge during SFA activities is the need to deny critical information about friendly intentions, capabilities, and activities to hostile elements. The nature of SFA implies that many HN officials and the populace will know of certain US activities as they occur. Criminal and insurgent groups may have members or sympathizers within HN institutions acting as informants. US and foreign personnel involved in SFA activities and programs should be provided extensive OPSEC training to ensure effectiveness of their operations.

For further information on OPSEC, see JP 3-13.3, Operations Security.

j. **Communications Security.** Communications security is essential throughout planning and execution of SFA activities. SFA personnel should be trained in the protection of sensitive communications equipment and cryptographic materials.

For further information on communications security, see JP 6-0, Joint Communications System.

k. **Lessons Learned.** It is important to document and integrate lessons learned to allow the commander to modify future operations and activities to fit the special circumstances and environment as SFA activities occur. It is also important to conduct comprehensive after-action reviews and reports, focusing on the specifics of the SFA activities, to gather this information as soon as possible after mission execution. The Joint Staff, Joint and Coalition Operational Analysis, Joint Center for International Security Force Assistance (JCISFA), the Services, and other USG departments' and agencies' lessons learned programs provide readily available sources of information to SFA planners and operators. The SOF Reporting System on the Joint Lessons Learned Information System can provide additional information on peacetime SFA missions.

For further information for specific reporting procedures, refer to Chairman of the Joint Chiefs of Staff Instruction 3150.25E, Joint Lessons Learned Program.

3. Human Rights

HN personnel should be vetted prior to engagement to ensure no members of the training audience have violated human rights. No assistance shall be furnished under the Foreign Assistance Act or the Arms Export Control Act to any unit of the security forces of a foreign country if the Secretary of State has credible information that such unit has committed a gross violation of human rights. To comply with the requirements of the Leahy Amendment, prior to training beginning, trainees must be vetted through post and DOS mechanisms. Once a unit or a group of individuals has been identified to be trained, a request for human rights vetting will be submitted to the appropriate country US embassy. Per A Guide to the Vetting Process, the DOS reference guide for Human Rights Vetting, a minimum of 10 working days is required for DOS to vet. However, more lead time raises the probability of successfully vetting candidates. If there are derogatory results, DOD will then make its own determination whether or not to proceed with the training. US law prohibits the USG from providing funds to the FSF of a foreign country if DOS has credible evidence that the foreign country or its agents have engaged in a consistent pattern of gross violations of internationally recognized human rights, unless the Secretary of State determines and reports that the government of such country is taking effective measures to bring the responsible FSF unit to justice (Title 22, USC, Section 2304). This language also may be found in the annual DOD appropriations acts and prohibits such funding unless all necessary steps have been taken or SecDef, in consultation with the Secretary of State, decides to waive the prohibition due to extraordinary circumstances. A site survey team may assist in gathering this information.

4. Countering Insider Threats

Nontraditional threats, such as the insider threat, can undermine SFA activities as well as the cohesion of US forces and FSF. Strategically, they can undermine the overall efforts of the international community. Tactically, the breakdown of trust, communication, and cooperation between HN and US forces can affect military capability. Eliminating and/or minimizing the insider threat, especially by proper preparation and training of forces, is critical to mission success. However, more stringent force protection controls and measures that are overtly heavy handed must be well balanced yet culturally sensitive enough to not send the wrong message to the very people and organizations the US is trying to assist. Adversaries may view attacks against US forces as a particularly effective tactic, especially when using co-opted HN forces to conduct these attacks. While these types of "insider" or "green on blue" attacks have been context-specific to a particular theater, JFCs should nevertheless ensure that their force protection plans take into account the potential for these types of attacks and plan appropriate countermeasures as the situation dictates. To reduce the potential for insider attacks, FSF should be further vetted to identify individuals whose motivations toward the HN and USG are in question.

5. Defense and Non-Defense Security Sector Security Force Assistance

a. **Defense Activities That Are Not SFA.** US forces may also conduct other activities with HN defense forces that do not clearly provide a direct contribution to the capability and capacity of the FSF, and therefore are not SFA activities. These might include military-to-military contacts whose purpose is simply to negotiate access or status agreements. Many senior leader engagements, wherein senior US military leaders meet with senior officers of the HN military, ministry of defense (MOD), or other officers of the HN government, are military engagement or SC activities, but not SFA activities, because they establish or reaffirm relationships or enhance US access to HN ports, airfields, or infrastructure. Despite their classification as something other than SFA activities, it is important to also understand that other SC activities are part of comprehensive USG effort to achieve the military objectives and reach the end state expressed in the TCP, country plan, or a contingency plan.

b. **Non-Defense Security Sector Activities.** Department of Defense Instruction (DODI) 5000.68, *Security Force Assistance,* has a provision that DOD, if required, and to the extent authorized by law, supports the development of the capability and capacity of non-defense ministry security forces and their supporting institutions." In general, existing US statutes prohibit DOD participation in developmental activities. Not all HNs have chosen to organize themselves in strict accordance with US organizational structures. Some HNs do not have a MOD, yet they field security forces. Examples of these non-MOD security forces include paramilitary police (gendarmerie, carabinieri), border guards, state and national police, coast guard-type forces or coastal defense forces, customs agents, counter narcotics force, and ministry of interior.

(1) DOD has several capabilities that may be of significant value in developing the capability and capacity of these non-MOD security forces. As GCCs develop TCPs and country plans to support their theater strategy and objectives, and in coordination with the applicable COMs and country teams, GCCs should identify capability and capacity gaps in these non-MOD forces and include proposals to address them. However, DOD will not execute or support such activities without proper authority.

(2) In most cases, another interagency partner will have primary responsibility and legal authority to work with HNs to develop capability and capacity of these non-MOD security forces. With proper coordination and approval, the GCC can provide DOD personnel and units with unique skill sets not available to other agencies to assist in this development activity under the supervision and/or authority of the lead USG agency. In some situations, other interagency partners may have specific skills to develop non-MOD security force capabilities and capacities, but do not have sufficient personnel available to meet requirements. Again, with proper coordination and authorization, this effort can involve tasking DOD personnel to assist in this effort.

(3) In some situations, other interagency partners may have the appropriate skills and personnel, but existing security conditions may prevent their use. In those environments, subject to proper coordination and authorization, DOD may be required to develop those non-MOD security capabilities or capacity. The GCC should make provisions for transition of responsibilities to other interagency partners as the security situation allows.

6. Other Operations and Activities

a. There are activities which are part of overall DOD security cooperation efforts that provide valuable opportunities for engagements between the US and HNs, but fall outside the scope of SFA. Regardless, these additional activities should be planned and executed by GCCs using DOD individuals and units, and will have significant impact and effect on SFA activities. In some cases, these SC activities may provide support to military and MOD security forces, but do not contribute directly to building capability or capacity within the FSF.

b. Example activities might include:

(1) DDR. DDR is typically a feature of post-conflict operations. It contributes to stabilizing the security environment, but is not a direct contribution to capability and capacity.

(2) Foreign humanitarian assistance.

(3) Medical civil action program exercises. These exercises can enhance the health of the population from whom recruits are drawn, but do not make direct contribution to capability and capacity.

c. The common thread throughout these activities is other interagency partners typically have lead responsibility to coordinate them with the HN's non-MOD, even non-security forces. The role for DOD personnel and units is limited to providing support (e.g., skills, logistics, transportation). These activities may contribute to the success of other SFA activities, but are not SFA activities themselves.

7. Support to Other Host Nation Institutions

a. Building capability and capacity of FSF, including their ministries and supporting institutions, will not likely succeed as an isolated, stand-alone program; it will be a whole of USG initiatives and programs. The GCC should participate or provide support to other USG efforts to create or modify conditions within the HN to support increased capability and capacity within the security sector.

b. **Rule of Law.** The rule of law in a country is characterized by just legal frameworks, public order, accountability to the law, access to justice, and a culture of lawfulness. Rule of law requires laws that are publicly promulgated, equally enforced, and independently adjudicated, and that are consistent with international human rights principles. Systems for enforcing civil order, the judiciary, law enforcement, penal and correctional systems, should also exist and function effectively. For example, in one country, US forces worked to train a coastal defense unit to patrol and enforce their economic exclusion zone waters, including fisheries. This HN unit successfully boarded a trawler with an illegal catch worth millions of dollars and escorted that detained trawler into port. However, adequate legal systems were not in place to charge and try the crew in a court of law, nor to handle the cargo of the trawler. Months later, the trawler remained in port with the full catch on board, but no ice or other refrigeration. As a result, a rotted catch, initially valuable, that could have been preserved, sold, or otherwise fed to the local populace. Had appropriate legal processes been in place, this unfortunate and wasteful outcome could instead have benefitted the local populace.

c. Other elements of government should also exist to support the increased capability and capacity of FSF and their supporting institutions. Adequate funding and economic and banking processes should exist and function effectively to allow for financial support of the security sector. Adequate transportation systems should also function effectively. For example, air traffic control, airfield navigation devices (24 hour, all-weather) might be required. Road, rail, and river distribution systems might be required to support adequate logistical support of FSF. The GCC should consider these and other developmental sectors and coordinate with the country team.

8. Operational and Tactical Levels of Security Force Assistance Effort

a. SFA will reside in a range of acceptability of the nation receiving the support and acceptability of the nation providing the support. The US conducts SFA where it aligns with US interests and the interests of the legitimate authority of the developing FSF. SFA activities focus instead on the operational and tactical fundamentals of placing policy into action. Primarily, this requires an understanding of FSF capabilities in order to address a legitimate authority's political problems. The FSF problems will reside in one of three functions, illustrated by Figure IV-1: executive direction, generate, or operate.

(1) **Executive/Ministerial/Service Direction.** Those activities that develop national policy for the FSF. This guidance forms, justifies, authorizes, and directs the parameters for the generating and employment of FSF.

(a) All security forces apply some level of executive direction, which empowers a generating and employing or operating function. The US separates these functions, with OSD, the Joint Staff, and elements of the Services providing the executive direction. The Services are also responsible for the majority of the generating function and GCCs are responsible for employing the operational forces. Subsequently, the ability to deploy resides primarily in the operational forces while the expertise to generate resides in fixed facilities and installations run by the Services.

(b) Executive functions regulate and resource both the operating and generating functions. These executive functions consist of practices, processes, and structures.

1. *Advise political leadership* by providing an understanding of problems and solutions in relation to security force issues. These may include, but are not limited to, force employment options, operational requirements, or military and political consequences of pending decisions.

2. *Policy* establishes the regulation of FSF in the context of the political purpose that department, agency, organization, Service, or unit serves.

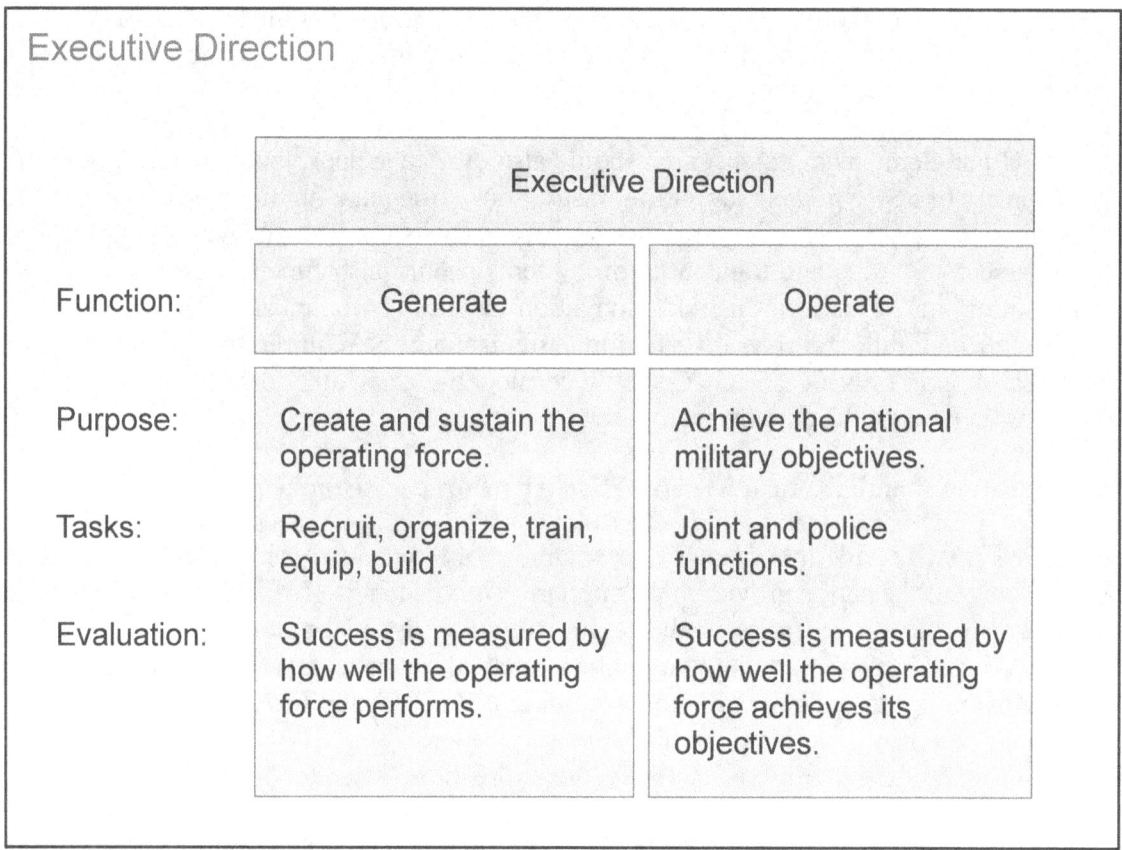

Figure IV-1. Executive Direction

<u>3.</u> *Strategic planning* supports formulation of security force plans to achieve a desired political end. Strategic planning encompasses not only the delivery and employment of operational forces, but also considers the required capabilities which should be generated and sustained to achieve those ends, as well as the associated second and third order effects.

<u>4.</u> *Assess readiness* to support identification of capability or capacity gaps as they relate to the functions, roles, and missions which security force departments, agencies, services, and organizations should perform in order to achieve a political purpose.

<u>5.</u> *Review and analysis* to provide insights into current or future capability and capacity gaps as they relate to fulfilling known or anticipated roles and missions for the security force. As a function, it requires the capability to collect and process relative information from operations, exercises, or experiments and then package and distribute the analysis in a manner useful to decision makers.

<u>6.</u> *Forecasting and budgeting* considers future requirements in both the operating and generating functions and requests or allocates resources to meet the anticipated priorities.

(2) **Generating Forces.** Primarily, this function includes organizing, recruiting/manning, training, equipping, mobilizing, servicing, and supplying FSF.

Fundamentally, this core function requires identification, resourcing, and resolution of capability gaps in the areas of doctrine, organization, training, materiel, leadership and education, personnel, facilities, policy, and Service and DOD equivalent policy of the FSF.

(a) As US generating force's staffing is generally singular and not deployable by design, this creates a problem for the operational force, which is often tasked during large-scale operations, to provide all the US capability to develop every aspect of an FSF. Through understanding of the demands being place on the force conducting SFA, commanders can take steps to mitigate shortages in generating expertise through training or augmentation.

(b) Generating functions develop and sustain capabilities in the operating functions. These practices, processes, and structures are:

1. *Recruiting.* Supports the selection and integration of non-security force personnel from outside Services, agencies, or organizations into its system as security force members. Normally, recruiting is the first step for a prospective member and precedes an accessions compatibility examination, and some form of individual training, which further integrates them into the security force. Recruiting is a key force generation function as it sustains the organization with the personnel required to maintain its force levels.

2. *Organizing.* Supports mobilization/demobilization, force management, resourcing, distribution, or other efforts that support the forming or reforming of units and supporting organizations required to generate and sustain capabilities that meet operational requirements.

3. *Training.* Supports the development and sustainment of systems that provide the resources (doctrine, materiel, funds, terrain, time, personnel, regulations) required to identify, achieve, and sustain a level of training readiness to meet operational requirements.

4. *Equipping.* Develops, tests, fields, distributes, and maintains the materiel required for security force personnel and organizations to train and execute those tasks associated with their roles and missions.

5. *Building.* Develops and maintains the physical infrastructure required to generate forces. This may include installations, ranges, buildings, road networks, airfields, shipyards, or other security force-related infrastructure.

(3) **Operating Forces.** Employ or operate as it applies to FSF, includes collective training and performing missions assigned to the unit. This includes integration of the FSF's operational functions such as the joint functions, consisting of *maneuver, intelligence, fires, force protection, sustainment,* and *command and control* during actual operations. Employment, as it applies to police security forces, may include training and actual operations with the integration of *patrolling, forensics, apprehension, intelligence, investigations, incarceration, communications,* and *sustainment.*

9. Inter-Relationships of the Three Functional Components of Foreign Security Forces

a. For illustrative purposes, this discussion uses the joint functions found in JP 3-0, *Joint Operations,* as a guide to consider FSF functions. These functions are broad enough to be applicable in part or in whole to any security force that is employed to attain end states and uses familiar terms to communicate capabilities. Planners may use other descriptions as required, but should include sufficient detail to associate tasks and supporting capabilities to assist FSF.

b. It is important to consider all three functional FSF components in the context of the development of FSF capabilities. All three components perform tasks that sustain the generation and employment of those capabilities. The objectives assigned to the FSF functional components help define both the purpose each serves and a desired condition of a sustainable security force and its capabilities.

c. Within the context of a sustainable FSF, it is now possible to visualize and describe the relationships between the three functional types of FSF. The executive direction encompasses and runs in the background as it regulates and resources both the generating and operating forces. The executive direction function provides leadership in the context of the political purpose the security force serves. The generating function exists to support the operating function with the capabilities required to conduct the range of tasks associated with its missions. The operating function should provide feedback on changes in objectives and conditions, which informs and supports needed changes in the generating function.

d. A given security force may combine some or all of the three functions in an organization or they may be separated. This depends upon the nature of the security force and the political purposes it serves. Functional relationships may change due to geography, time, political realignment, or other circumstances. This framework provides a brief understanding of SFA as it relates to developing FSF capabilities and capacities. The intention is not to develop a campaign design or planning template. Rather, it is a tool for visualizing and understanding relationships in an FSF.

APPENDIX A
REFERENCES

The development of this JDN is based upon the following primary references.

1. Federal Statutory Laws

    a. Title 10, USC.

    b. Title 22, USC.

    c. Title 32, USC.

2. Strategic Guidance and Policy

    a. *The National Security Strategy of the United States of America.*

    b. *National Defense Strategy of the United States of America.*

    c. *National Military Strategy.*

    d. *National Strategy for Homeland Security.*

    e. *Joint Strategic Capabilities Plan.*

3. Department of Defense Publications

    a. DODI 2205.02, *Humanitarian and Civic Assistance (HCA) Activities.*

    b. DODI 3000.05, *Stability Operations.*

    c. DODI 5000.68, *Security Force Assistance.*

    d. Department of Defense Directive (DODD) 3000.07, *Irregular Warfare.*

    e. DODD 5132.03, *DOD Policy and Responsibilities Relating to Security Cooperation.*

    f. Secretary of Defense Memorandum, *Joint Center for International Security Force Assistance (JCISFA) Charter.*

4. Joint Publications

    a. JP 1-02, *DOD Dictionary of Military and Associated Terms.*

    b. JP 3-0, *Joint Operations.*

    c. JP 3-05, *Special Operations.*

    d. JP 3-07, *Stability Operations.*

e. JP 3-13.2, *Military Information Support Operations.*

f. JP 3-22, *Foreign Internal Defense.*

g. JP 3-24, *Counterinsurgency Operations.*

h. JP 3-26, *Counterterrorism.*

i. JP *3-57, Civil Military Operations.*

5. Other

a. *Security Force Assistance Introductory Guide, USSOCOM, 28 July 2011.*

b. *Commander's Handbook for Security Force Assistance, JCISFA, July 2008.*

c. *Security Sector Reform, USAID, DOD, DOS, March 2009.*

GLOSSARY
PART I—ABBREVIATIONS AND ACRONYMS

AOR	area of responsibility
CCDR	combatant commander
CEW	civilian expeditionary workforce
CF	conventional forces
COIN	counterinsurgency
COM	chief of mission
DCM	deputy chief of mission
DDR	disarmament, demobilization, and reintegration
DOD	Department of Defense
DODD	Department of Defense directive
DODI	Department of Defense instruction
DOS	Department of State
FID	foreign internal defense
FMF	foreign military financing
FMS	foreign military sales
FSF	foreign security forces
GCC	geographic combatant commander
GEF	Guidance for Employment of the Force
HN	host nation
HNS	host-nation support
IDAD	internal defense and development
IGO	intergovernmental organization
IMET	international military education and training
IO	information operations
JCISFA	Joint Center for International Security Force Assistance
JDN	joint doctrine note
JFC	joint force commander
JP	joint publication
JSCP	Joint Strategic Capabilities Plan
MISO	military information support operations
MOD	ministry of defense
MOE	measures of effectiveness
MOP	measures of performance
MTT	mobile training team

NGO	nongovernmental organization
OPSEC	operations security
OSD	Office of the Secretary of Defense
OTERA	organize, train, equip, rebuild/build, advise
PA	public affairs
PM	Bureau of Political-Military Affairs (DOS)
PN	partner nation
SA	security assistance
SC	security cooperation
SDO/DATT	senior defense official/defense attaché
SecDef	Secretary of Defense
SFA	security force assistance
SOF	special operations forces
SSR	security sector reform
TCP	theater campaign plan
UN	United Nations
USAID	United States Agency for International Development
USC	United States Code
USCG	United States Coast Guard
USG	United States Government
USSOCOM	United States Special Operations Command

PART II—TERMS AND DEFINITIONS

foreign security forces. All organizations and their personnel that are under governmental control with the mission of protecting a government, an organization or people from internal and/or external threats. Also called **FSF.**

www.ingramcontent.com/pod-product-compliance
Lightning Source LLC
Chambersburg PA
CBHW081750280526
45789CB00008B/2799